The

CUPBOARD TO TABLE

Cookbook

The
CUPBOARD
TO TABLE
Cookbook

Satisfying Meals Made from
What You Have on Hand

JUDY HANNEMANN

The Countryman Press
A division of W. W. Norton & Company
Independent Publishers Since 1923

For information about permission to reproduce selections from this book, write to Permissions, The Countryman Press, 500 Fifth Avenue, New York, NY 10110

For information about special discounts for bulk purchases, please contact W. W. Norton Special Sales at specialsales@wwnorton.com or 800-233-4830

Manufacturing by Quad/Graphics, Taunton
Book design by Chin-Yee Lai

Library of Congress Cataloging-in-Publication Data

Names: Hannemann, Judy, author.
Title: The cupboard to table cookbook : satisfying meals made from what you have on hand / Judy Hannemann.
Description: Woodstock, VT : The Countryman Press, 2016. | Includes bibliographical references and index.
Identifiers: LCCN 2015046470 | ISBN 9781581574012 (hardcover : alk. paper)
Subjects: LCSH: Quick and easy cooking. | LCGFT: Cookbooks.
Classification: LCC TX833.5 .H354 2016 | DDC 641.5/12—dc23
LC record available at http://lccn.loc.gov/2015046470

The Countryman Press
www.countrymanpress.com

A division of W. W. Norton & Company, Inc.
500 Fifth Avenue, New York, NY 10110
www.wwnorton.com

10 9 8 7 6 5 4 3 2 1

To David S. Cadby, my "Mini Me."

CONTENTS

INTRODUCTION...ix

SIMPLY GOOD SNACKS & STARTERS...3

QUICK & HEARTY MAINS...23

EASY-PEASY SOUPS & SIDES...87

BEST NO-FUSS BREADS & MUFFINS...119

SWEETEST-EVER HAPPY ENDINGS...145

P.S. DON'T FORGET THE DRINKS!...195

INDEX...205

INTRODUCTION

I love to cook. And I love to share food and recipes with friends and family. I enjoy trying out new ingredients, experimenting with flavors, spending time perfecting culinary techniques, and expanding my gourmet repertoire. But like most of us, I have those days when I don't want to fuss. Even as a retiree, I still have those busy "crunch" times in my schedule when I can't fit in even a quick trip to the grocery store. And I know that for many who are on a limited budget, be they students or retirees or families trying to make ends meet, those final days of each month can be a challenge when trying to prepare delicious, satisfying meals with only the last length of a shoe-string in the pocketbook.

For me, having a well-stocked cupboard is second nature, a must in maintaining a food blog. I live in a rural area where there is no supermarket or convenience store nearby, so running around the corner to pick up a missing ingredient is never an option for me. Keeping your cupboard well stocked doesn't mean spending a fortune either. Two or three times per year, I load up at a big-box discount grocery in my area for all the essential shelf-stable items. And I use my freezer to take advantage of sales on meat, poultry, butter, and frozen veggies.

Friends and neighbors, some of whom use their Catskill houses as second homes for weekends and holidays, have often told me how much they appreciate my ready ideas for effortless meals served up in a jiffy. These are recipes that encourage relaxation, call for simple, nutritious ingredients, and say, "Just kick back tonight and enjoy the Mountain View."

So, for the busy, budget-minded, and everyday cook in need of a break from lengthy recipes and extensive food preparation, as well as for the rural chef, minimalist cabin dweller, and relaxed weekender, this book will come in handy. Here are over 100 out-of-the-cupboard recipes to please everyone at your table, all economical and made from supplies most people will already have available—no so-called "fancy" ingredients required.

Making meals from convenient items is not haute cuisine, but it is a practical, fun, and easy way to enjoy tasty, nourishing food on your own or together with family and friends. Many of the recipes in this book are fan favorites, the go-to comfort foods of choice for fellow readers of my blog. I hope they will become some of your favorites too.

ITEMS FOR A WELL-STOCKED PANTRY

I make sure to keep these items on hand in my own pantry,
which have been used in this book's recipes.

The Spice/Herb and Condiment Shelf

Table salt

Kosher salt

Ground black pepper

White & black whole peppercorns

Thyme

Basil

Oregano

Parsley

Chives

Poultry seasoning

Sage

Garlic powder

Soy sauce

Chicken stock cubes

Beef stock cubes

Taco seasoning

Chili powder

Dehydrated onion flakes

Ground cinnamon

Ground nutmeg

Ground cloves

Olive oil

Vegetable oil

Plain breadcrumbs

Ketchup

Chili sauce

Mayonnaise

Grated shelf-stable Parmesan cheese

The Baking Shelf

Flour

Granulated sugar

Brown sugar

Confectioner's sugar

Baking powder

Baking soda

Active dry yeast

Vanilla extract

Almond extract

Honey

Chocolate chips

Cornmeal

Cocoa

Flaked coconut

Raisins

Peanut butter

Cornstarch

Baking (unsweetened) chocolate

Caramel sauce (ice cream–topping kind)

Assorted jams and jellies

Vanilla instant pudding

Chocolate instant pudding

Graham crackers

The Grain, Rice, and Pasta Shelf

Long-grain white rice

Jasmine rice

Quinoa

Spaghetti

Elbow macaroni

Orzo

Flour/corn tortillas

Egg noodles

Pearl (Israeli) couscous

Regular couscous

Canned Goods Shelf

Canned peaches

Canned apricots

Canned crushed pineapple

Canned pineapple juice

Apple pie filling

Cherry pie filling

Canned corn (kernel & creamed)

Cream of mushroom soup

Cream of chicken soup

Cheddar cheese soup

Evaporated milk

Condensed milk

Canned whole potatoes

Canned kidney/cannellini beans

Canned pumpkin purée

Canned pastry fillings

Canned mushrooms

Refrigerated Dairy Shelf

Milk

Heavy cream

Light cream

Cheddar cheese

Swiss cheese

Asiago cheese

Cream cheese

Eggs

Butter

Greek yogurt

Biscuits

Crescent dough

Pizza dough

Freezer Stock Shelf

Chicken (whole, parts)

Ground beef

Pork chops

Italian sausage

Bulk breakfast sausage

Shrimp

Bacon

Beef roasts

Puff pastry

Frozen berries

Mashed bananas

Orange juice concentrate

The
CUPBOARD
TO TABLE
Cookbook

SIMPLY GOOD SNACKS & STARTERS

BACON BOMBS

Who doesn't love bacon and savory cream cheese? You'll find both in these easy to-make snacks. The original recipe uses refrigerated biscuits—use them if you have them on hand. But if you don't—there's always baking mix!

Serves: 16–18

Ingredients

1 cup baking mix (like Bisquick)

1 tablespoon minced fresh chives (or 1 teaspoon dry)

⅓ cup milk

2 ounces cream cheese (this measure is approximate)

1 scallion, chopped very finely

8–9 slices of bacon

oil for frying

Instructions

1. Mix baking mix and chives together. Add milk and stir until dough forms a ball. Depending on atmospheric conditions, you may need a drop or 2 more milk.

2. Turn dough out onto a lightly floured surface and knead a few times. Roll out dough about ¼-inch thick and cut out biscuits. The diameter of my biscuits is about 2½ inches. Cut each biscuit in half.

3. Mix the cream cheese with the chopped scallion. Put about 1 teaspoon of cream cheese mixture in the center of each biscuit half. Seal the biscuit dough well around the cream cheese and roll into a ball.

4. Cut bacon slices in half. Wrap a half bacon slice around each biscuit ball and secure with skewer.

5. Heat about 2 inches of oil in a deep saucepan to 375°F. Fry about 4 to 5 "bombs" at a time for about 10 minutes total, turning once. Remove with a slotted spoon and place on a paper towel-lined plate. These may be kept warm in a 200°F oven while frying subsequent batches.

CHEESY PRETZEL BITES

This is for those who love the most famous of NYC street foods—soft pretzels. Make these and watch them disappear, because they are just too good. The pretzel dough is very soft and a bit fussy to work with, but the end product is worth it. Substitute any cheese you have on hand for the filling.

Serves: 9

Ingredients

Cheesy Pretzel Bites

2 ½ cups flour

½ teaspoon salt

1 teaspoon sugar

1 cup warm water

2 ¼ teaspoon yeast

36 ¼-inch cubes of Velveeta

Baking Soda Wash

½ tablespoon baking soda

½ cup very hot water

Instructions

1. In a heavy stand mixer, place all ingredients, except for Velveeta, and mix with paddle attachment until well blended.

2. Change to dough hook and knead for 5 minutes, or until dough becomes elastic and less sticky. You may have to add a bit more flour to achieve this texture. If you don't have a mixer with a dough hook, mix all ingredients together, turn out onto a floured surface, and knead for 5 minutes.

3. Cover dough and let rest for 30 minutes. Punch down dough.

4. Preheat oven to 450°F. Line a baking sheet with parchment or grease. Mix the baking soda and hot water. Set aside.

5. Break off 36 equal portions of the dough and slightly flatten.

6. Put a cube of Velveeta in the center and seal well, forming into a ball.

7. When all balls are formed, roll in the baking soda wash and place on prepared baking sheet.

8. Bake at 450°F for 10 to 15 minutes or until balls start to turn golden brown. You can brush with a bit of melted butter during the last 5 minutes of baking if you wish.

COCONUT SHRIMP

Close your eyes and pop one of these delicious shrimp in your mouth and taste the Caribbean Islands! This versatile recipe could be an appetizer or a main course.

Serves: 3–4

Ingredients

1 pound large shrimp, tail left on

½ cup, plus 2 tablespoons flour

1 teaspoon baking powder

1 teaspoon salt

½ teaspoon cayenne pepper

1 egg

⅓ cup ice water

1 cup shredded coconut

oil for frying

Instructions

1. Place enough oil in a deep, heavy skillet to reach about 1 inch up the sides. Alternatively, you can use a deep fryer.

2. Heat oil to 375°F—a cube of bread should brown in 1 minute if oil is the correct temperature.

3. Remove shells and vein from shrimp, but leave tail on as it makes it convenient for dipping.

4. In a small bowl, mix the flour, baking powder, salt, cayenne, and egg.

5. Add just enough of the ice water to make a thick batter that will cling to the shrimp.

6. Place shredded coconut on a flat plate, dip shrimp in batter, then coat with coconut.

7. Place shrimp in hot oil and deep fry for about 3 to 5 minutes on each side, or until golden brown.

8. Remove to parchment-covered plate to keep warm if frying another batch.

GARLIC LIME WINGS

The perfect balance of flavors makes these wings a real treat. Serve them up for tailgating or any party. They're sure to be a hit with any garlic lover and offer a change of pace from the usual lemon-based flavor.

Serves: 6–8

Ingredients

3–4 pounds chicken wings

2 teaspoons salt

½ teaspoon pepper

½ teaspoon garlic powder

Sauce:

Juice of 1 whole lime

½ teaspoon lime zest

½ cup honey or dark corn syrup

4 garlic cloves, finely minced

¼ teaspoon chipotle-flavored hot sauce (optional)

Instructions

1. Split wings, cutting through joint. Discard wing tips.

2. Preheat oven to 400°F. Lightly spray a large baking sheet with non-stick spray.

3. Mix the salt, pepper, and garlic powder together. Place wings, skin side up, on prepared baking sheet. Sprinkle with the salt mixture.

4. Bake at 400°F for 30 to 40 minutes.

5. Mix all sauce ingredients in a small bowl. Brush liberally on cooked wings.

6. You can pop them under the broiler for a couple minutes to brown the sauce, but it's not necessary. Leftover sauce can be used for dipping.

HOT ASIAGO SPINACH DIP

The robust flavor of Asiago cheese dominates this hot cheese dip. If you need a substitute, choose another robust, hard cheese—either Parmesan or Romano. Serve this one up with a good cracker—and yes, Saltines will do—and the party is on!

Serves: 8–10

Ingredients

1 10-ounce package frozen chopped spinach, thawed

4 ounces cream cheese, softened and cut in small cubes

2 large garlic cloves, minced

¼ cup mayonnaise

¼ cup sour cream or Greek yogurt

2 tablespoons chopped flat-leaf parsley

2 cups shredded Asiago cheese

Instructions

1. Preheat oven to 350°F. Lightly grease or spray a 1-quart gratin dish or any 1-quart casserole dish.

2. Squeeze out as much water from the spinach as you can. Place in a large bowl and combine with the cream cheese, garlic, mayonnaise, sour cream, parsley, and 1½ cups of the Asiago cheese. If you wish, you may use an electric mixer to combine. Otherwise, small lumps of cream cheese will remain in the mixture—I don't mind this, but if you want a very smooth dip, then it's best to use the electric mixer.

3. Top with remaining ½ cup of Asiago.

4. Bake at 350°F for 25 to 30 minutes, or until bubbly around the edges.

5. Pop under the broiler for a few minutes to brown the top.

6. Serve with a sliced baguette, crackers, or chips.

PARMESAN GARLIC SNACK MIX

Be warned: Highly addictive snacking ahead! This mix has a more intense flavor than the usual cereal-based snack mixes. Plus, it uses ingredients most folks have on hand.

Serves: 6

Ingredients

4 cups Chex-style cereal (any variety)

2 cups pretzel sticks

2 cups small crackers

6 tablespoons butter

1 tablespoon garlic powder

¼–½ cup grated Parmesan or Romano cheese

Salt to taste

Instructions

1. Preheat oven to 300°F. Line a large baking sheet with foil; set aside.

2. Mix the cereal, pretzels, and crackers in a large bowl.

3. Melt the butter, either in the microwave or on the stovetop. Add the garlic powder to the butter and stir to combine.

4. Drizzle the butter mixture evenly over cereal mixture. Stir well, making sure the pieces are coated with garlic butter.

5. Stir in desired amount of cheese. Spread on baking sheet.

6. Bake for 30 minutes, stirring midway through cook time. Alternatively, the snack mix may be placed in a slow cooker set on high. Cook for 1 hour, stirring every 15 minutes. Reduce temperature to warm, add salt, and serve mix directly from the pot.

POT STICKERS

You don't have to bother with takeout ever again! Did you know pot stickers are easy to make and the dough is just flour and hot water? Everyone has those ingredients on hand and you can fill this dough with anything you like. You're not locked into the standard ground pork filling in the recipe!

Makes: 48 dumplings

Ingredients

Pot Sticker Filling:

6 ounces Napa (celery) cabbage, or regular green cabbage

3 teaspoons coarse salt (divided)

1 pound ground pork

¼ cup finely chopped green onion—both the white and green part

1 tablespoon finely chopped cilantro or ½ teaspoon dried

1 large garlic clove, minced very finely

1 teaspoon cornstarch

½ teaspoon sesame oil

1 tablespoon soy sauce

⅛ teaspoon grated fresh ginger or a pinch of dried

1 tablespoon dry sherry

Vegetable oil, for frying

Pot Sticker Dough:

2 cups flour

1 cup boiling water

Dipping Sauce (optional):

1 cup soy sauce

½ teaspoon sesame oil

2 tablespoons honey

Instructions

1. For the filling, finely shred the cabbage and sprinkle with 2 teaspoons of the coarse salt and toss. Set aside for 5 minutes.

2. Mix the meat and remaining ingredients plus the leftover 1 teaspoon coarse salt in a medium bowl. Squeeze out the water from the shredded cabbage and add to meat mixture, mixing well. Set aside.

3. For the dough, mix the flour and boiling water until a soft dough forms. Turn out onto floured work surface and knead until smooth and elastic, about 5 minutes. Cut dough in half. Roll each half into a 12-inch roll. Cut ½-inch portions of dough from the roll. Roll each ½-inch portion into a 3-inch circle. Place about 1 tablespoon of filling in each circle.

   NOTE: I roll out ALL my dough circles before I begin to fill them—the process is cleaner and more efficient.

5. Bring the edges of the circles up and seal very well, pinching to pleat slightly. This will form a crescent-shaped dumpling They can be shaped other ways, but I find that to be a complete pain and the crescent shape is the one most commonly found In restaurants.

6. Heat a large skillet over medium-high heat. Add about 1 tablespoon vegetable oil if using a regular pan, or ½ tablespoon if using a nonstick pan. When oil is very hot, add the dumplings, pleat side up in the pan. Fry for about 3 to 5 minutes, or until the bottoms are golden brown and start to crisp. Add ½ cup water, cover, reduce heat to medium, and steam until all water is absorbed; about 5 to 7 minutes.

7. If using the dipping sauce, put all ingredients in a small saucepan and heat, stirring, until honey is dissolved.

   NOTE: Dumplings can be made ahead of time, then frozen and reheated before serving.

PEPPERONI PIZZA PULL-APART

If the family is crying out for pizza, here's a quick fix that will fit the bill nicely. No delivery required because this recipe uses what you already have on hand. No refrigerated pizza dough in the tube? Make your own from ingredients already in your cupboard!

Serves: 8

Ingredients

2 tubes (13.8 ounces) refrigerated pizza dough

8 ounces sliced pepperoni

2 cups shredded mozzarella cheese

¼ cup grated Parmesan

2 tablespoons diced sun-dried tomatoes

2 tablespoons chopped fresh parsley, or 1 tablespoon dried

1 teaspoon garlic powder

1 teaspoon oregano

½ teaspoon basil

⅓ cup extra-virgin olive oil

Pizza sauce for dipping

Instructions

Note: May also be made in a Bundt pan.

1. Preheat oven to 350°F. Spray a 9 x 13-inch pan with cooking spray. Set aside.

2. Open tubes of pizza crust but *do not* unroll. Cut into 1-inch pieces (that resemble pre-cut biscuits), then cut each circle into quarters.

3. Cut pepperoni slices into quarters as well.

4. Place all ingredients, except olive oil and pizza sauce, in a large bowl and toss well to combine. Drizzle with the olive oil and toss so that all the pizza dough is coated with oil.

5. Turn dough onto prepared pan, distributing evenly.

6. Bake for 30 to 35 minutes, or until golden brown on top and dough in the center is cooked.

7. Serve with pizza sauce for dipping.

STATE FAIR CORN DOGS

America's most beloved state-fair snack easily made at home! These cornmeal-coated hot dogs please kids of all ages. Make them with mini hot dogs for an appetizer at your next get-together.

Serves: 8

Ingredients

Oil for deep-frying

1 cup yellow cornmeal

1 cup flour

1 tablespoon baking powder

⅛ teaspoon cayenne pepper

½ teaspoon salt

2 eggs

1 cup milk

1 tablespoon sugar

1 tablespoon honey

8 hot dogs (any brand, any type of meat)

Cornstarch or flour for dusting hot dogs

8 candy-apple sticks

Instructions

1. Pour enough oil in a deep sauté pan or skillet to reach a height of about 2 to 3 inches. Heat oil over medium heat until it reaches 375°F.

2. Mix cornmeal, flour, baking powder, cayenne pepper, and salt in a medium bowl.

3. In a separate bowl beat egg with the milk, sugar, and honey until the sugar is dissolved.

4. Add the wet ingredients to the dry ingredients and stir until the batter is smooth. Transfer part of the batter to a tall glass (like a Tom Collins or iced tea glass), leaving at least an inch between the batter and the top of the glass.

5. Dry hot dogs by rolling on a paper towel. Dust the hot dogs with flour or cornstarch. Insert a candy-apple stick into the hot dog, leaving about 1 to 2 inches of the stick outside the meat.

6. Dip a hot dog in the batter, holding on to the exposed stick. Let some batter drain, and place in hot oil. Repeat with 2 more hot dogs (don't fry more than 3 at one time). Fry until golden brown, turning once or twice with tongs.

7. Remove to plate lined with paper towels. Repeat until all hot dogs are fried.

8. May be kept warm in a 200°F oven. These also freeze well.

TACO CUPS

Tacos shaped like muffins make this family meal something different. This shape also makes them an excellent appetizer to serve at your next party or tailgate.

Makes: 24 taco cups

Ingredients

1 pound lean ground beef

1 small onion, chopped

1 package (1.25 ounces) taco seasoning

1 can (16 ounces) refried beans

2 cups shredded Mexican blend cheese

1 package (12 ounces) wonton skins

½ cup sliced ripe olives

3 green onions, sliced thinly

Instructions

1. Preheat oven to 350°F. Grease or spray 2 dozen muffin cups.

2. Brown ground beef and onion over medium heat; drain any fat.

3. Add taco seasoning, refried beans, and ½ cup of the cheese. Set aside.

4. Line each muffin cup with 3 wonton skins, overlapping so points are at 10, 2, and 6 o'clock (not absolutely necessary, but it looks nice and makes a more solid "cup").

5. Fill each cup with ground beef mixture, distributing approximately equal amounts in each cup.

6. Top each cup with remaining cheese.

7. Bake a 350°F for 15 to 20 minutes or until cheese is melted and wonton cups begin to get golden brown.

8. Garnish with olives and sliced green onion.

QUICK & HEARTY MAINS

BACON CHEESEBURGER MEATLOAF

Can't decide between meatloaf and cheeseburgers? Combine them in this great-tasting meatloaf! Don't want to bother with the latticed bacon? Just lay strips across the top!

Serves: 6–8

Ingredients

2 pounds extra-lean ground beef

¾ cup plain breadcrumbs

2 eggs

¼ cup chopped onion

1 teaspoon garlic powder

1 teaspoon salt

½ teaspoon pepper

1 tablespoon Worcestershire sauce, or steak sauce

1–2 tablespoons ketchup (use 1 tablespoon if using steak sauce)

1 cup Cheddar cheese, cut into ¼–½-inch cubes

8–10 slices bacon*

* I make a lattice with 8 slices of bacon to top the meatloaf—4 across, 4 down. You can use less bacon if you don't want to get fancy, but the loaf should be topped with bacon.

Instructions:

1. Preheat oven to 375°F.

2. In a large bowl, mix all ingredients except the bacon. Form into a loaf shape.

3. Top with either a fancy bacon lattice, or lay strips across the top. Make sure to tuck the bacon under the bottom of the meatloaf.

4. Place in an oblong pan (I used 7 x 11 inches with a rack) and bake for 50 to 60 minutes or until internal temperature is 160°F.

CLASSIC POT ROAST

Pot roast is the #1 American Sunday dinner. Everyone makes it differently, but here's my take on the classic version. And the ingredients are basic pantry items!

Serves: 4–8, depending on size of the roast

Ingredients

1 can (10.5-ounce) cream of mushroom soup

1 package (0.87-ounce) brown gravy mix (or 2 tablespoons if you buy bulk)

1 tablespoon dry instant onion soup mix

1 cup mushrooms, sliced (optional)

2 beef stock cubes

2 garlic cloves, crushed

1 cup water

1 small bay leaf (optional)

3–5 pounds beef roast (like bottom round, rump, or your choice)

Instructions:

1. Mix all ingredients, except beef roast in a small bowl. Set aside.

2. Place beef roast in the crock of a 5 to 6 quart slow cooker. Pour soup mixture over roast.

3. Cover and cook on low for 6 to 10 hours. Gravy may be thickened with flour/water or cornstarch/water, if desired.

DELUXE SKILLET TACO PIE

Less mess, more flavor! This taco pie has the great smoky flavor of chipotle right in the mix. Less mess at the table than conventional tacos; less cleanup because it cooks in one pan!

Serves: 4

Ingredients

1 pound extra-lean ground beef

1 medium onion, chopped

1 package taco seasoning

1 large chipotle (in adobo), chopped very finely

1 can (4-ounce) chopped green chilis

1 ½ cups shredded Cheddar cheese

½ cup baking mix (like Bisquick)

2 eggs

2 tablespoons salsa (mild, medium, or hot)

¾ cup milk

Instructions

1. Preheat oven to 400°F.

2. Brown ground beef and onion in a large (10-inch) heavy, oven-safe skillet; drain off any fat. Stir in taco seasoning.

3. Stir in chopped chipotle. Top with green chilis and ½ cup of the cheese.

4. In a small bowl, combine the baking mix, eggs, salsa, and milk. Beat well to combine. Pour over meat mixture in skillet.

5. Bake for 25 to 30 minutes or until knife inserted at the center of the pie comes out clean.

6. Top with remaining cheese and bake an additional 5 to 10 minutes. Let stand 5 minutes before slicing.

TAKEOUT BEEF FRIED RICE

Put down the phone! Don't call takeout! This fried rice is authentic, and you have most of the flavoring ingredients right on your shelf!

Serves: 6–8

Ingredients

4 cups cold, cooked jasmine rice

3 tablespoons oil (for frying egg)

3 eggs, lightly beaten

8 ounces lean ground beef*

2 garlic cloves, minced

2 tablespoons soy sauce, plus ¼ cup for later use

1 thin slice fresh ginger, crushed

2 tablespoons dry sherry or mirin (sweet saki)

1 teaspoon dark sesame oil

2 teaspoons sugar

4 sliced green onions, divided

*Any cooked leftover meat will do nicely as well. Use about 1 cup.

Instructions

1. Separate any clumps in the cold rice. Set aside.

2. In a very large skillet, sauté pan or wok, heat oil over high heat.

3. Add eggs and scramble, breaking up into smaller pieces. Cook until firm. Remove from pan and set aside.

4. Brown ground beef, garlic, 2 tablespoons soy sauce, ginger, and sherry well over high heat in the same pan used for the eggs until there is no liquid or fat left from the meat. Remove and discard the slice of ginger.

5. Add the rice to the same pan as the meat, stirring to combine and heat the rice (use high heat here, too).

6. Add the ¼ cup soy sauce, sesame oil, cooked eggs, sugar, and half of the green onions. Add more soy sauce to taste if needed. Stir fry until heated through. Serve immediately and top with remaining green onion.

MEATBALL SUBS

You can make your own meatballs or use frozen—a great last-minute meal that tastes great.

Serves: 4

Ingredients

Mini Italian Meatballs:

1 pound lean ground beef
(I used 93%)

2 eggs

2–3 tablespoons grated
Asiago cheese

2 teaspoons dried onion,
or 1 tablespoon finely
chopped fresh

1 teaspoon salt

½ teaspoon pepper

2 teaspoons garlic powder

1 cup (or so) fresh soft
breadcrumbs

½ teaspoon oregano

Pinch of basil

1 tablespoon olive oil for
frying

For the Sandwiches:

4 sub rolls, about 6-inches
long

20 meatballs

1 cup pasta sauce, like a
marinara (if you like it really
saucy, use more sauce)

2 tablespoons olive oil

1 teaspoon parsley

1 tablespoon Parmesan or
Romano cheese

1 cup shredded mozzarella

Instructions

Mini Italian Meatballs:

1. Place all ingredients, except olive oil, in a medium bowl and mix well. Meat mixture will be pretty soft.

2. Form into meatballs about the size of a walnut. You should get approximately 20 meatballs.

3. Heat the olive oil in a large skillet over medium heat.

4. Brown meatballs on all sides.

5. Reduce heat, cover and cook 10 minutes, or until internal temperature is 160°F.

Preparing the Sandwiches:

1. Preheat oven to 400°F.

2. Spray a 9 x 13-inch pan with nonstick spray.

3. Place rolls in prepared pan with slits facing upward (if you cut the rolls yourself, only cut ¾ of the way through).

4. Place 5 meatballs in each roll then ¼ cup pasta sauce over the meatballs in each roll.

5. Brush the exposed parts of the rolls with olive oil and sprinkle with the parsley and cheese. Bake for 20 minutes.

6. Top each roll with ¼ cup of the shredded mozzarella (yes, you can add more cheese— *much* more if you want!).

7. Return to oven and bake for an additional 10 minutes, or until cheese is melted and bubbly.

ONE-SKILLET SALISBURY STEAK WITH BUTTER MERLOT SAUCE

Here's a comfort meal made a little fancier with the addition of wine in the gravy. If you don't want to use wine, beef stock may be substituted.

Serves: 6

Ingredients

Meat Patties:

1½ pounds lean ground beef

3 tablespoons onion, finely chopped

3 garlic cloves, finely minced

1 tablespoon Worcestershire sauce, or soy sauce

2 eggs

2 cups soft breadcrumbs

½ teaspoon salt

¼ teaspoon pepper

1 tablespoon oil

2 tablespoons water

Sauce:

2 tablespoons butter

1 cup mushrooms, sliced

1 sprig (about 4-inches) fresh rosemary, or ½ teaspoon dry

1 cup merlot or semi-dry red wine

⅓ cup heavy cream

Instructions:

1. Mix all meat patty ingredients, except the oil and water, in a large bowl. Form into 6 patties.

2. Heat oil in a large skillet over medium heat, then brown meat patties on both sides.

3. Reduce heat, add the 1 tablespoon water, cover and simmer for 15 to 20 minutes, or until meat is 160°F (medium-well) per a meat thermometer, then remove patties to a plate and cover with foil to keep warm.

4. Wipe out the skillet with paper towels and set over medium-high heat.

5. Add butter, and when butter begins to brown, add the mushrooms and rosemary sprig. Stir this constantly—you want the mushrooms to almost singe.

6. Add the merlot (or beef stock) and deglaze pan.

7. Continue cooking over medium-high heat until liquid is reduced by 50 percent. Remove rosemary, then reduce heat and stir in cream. Heat through.

8. Pour sauce over meat patties and serve immediately.

RUSTIC BEEF POT PIE

It's amazing what you can do with leftovers! This gastropub delight was created with gravy mix, leftover roast beef, and a single sheet of frozen puff pastry!

Serves: 4

Ingredients

1 sheet frozen puff pastry, thawed

1 pound beef sirloin, top round London broil, or leftover roast beef

2 tablespoons butter

2 cups fresh mushrooms, thickly sliced

1 cup pearl onions

½ teaspoon thyme

½ teaspoon pepper

1½ cups beef (brown) gravy*

1 egg, beaten

*You can use either canned, jarred, homemade, or the dry mix (made according to directions)

Instructions

1. Preheat oven to 400°F. Lightly spray or grease 4 large ramekins (9 to 10-ounce volume).

2. Unfold sheet of puff pastry and roll out to a 13-inch square. Cut the sheet into quarters. Lightly press 1 square of pastry into each ramekin, pressing up the sides. Let the corners hang over. Set aside.

3. Cut steak into cubes about ½ to ¾ of an inch. If using leftover beef, cut it the same way.

4. Heat a large skillet over medium heat. Add butter to the pan and melt.

5. Add the beef and brown. Add the mushrooms, onions, thyme, and pepper. Sauté for about 5 minutes. Stir in gravy.

6. Divide steak/gravy mixture evenly between the 4 pastry-lined ramekins. Pull up the corners and pinch the points to almost seal. Brush the pastry corners with the beaten egg.

7. Bake for 20 to 25 minutes, or until the pastry is a deep, golden brown.

SKILLET BEEF PASTA CAPRESE WITH FIRE-ROASTED TOMATOES

Here's a taste of summer you can have year round thanks to common shelf ingredients!

Serves: 4

Ingredients

1 pound ground beef

1 tablespoon dehydrated onion

1 teaspoon salt

½ teaspoon pepper

1 teaspoon garlic powder

¼ teaspoon oregano

1 cup penne pasta

1 cup water

1 can (15-ounce) fire-roasted diced tomatoes

¼ cup Parmesan cheese

½ cup shredded mozzarella

4–6 fresh basil leaves, torn

Instructions:

1. Heat 10-inch skillet over medium-high heat.

2. Add the ground beef and brown well; drain and wipe out pan with a paper towel. Return pan to heat, and add browned meat back to the pan.

3. Add the onion, salt, pepper, garlic powder, and oregano, combining well, then add the pasta and water.

4. Bring to a boil, cover and reduce heat to low.

5. Cook for about 15 to 20 minutes, or until the water has been absorbed by the pasta.

6. Add the can of fire-roasted tomatoes (do not drain) and heat through.

7. Top with Parmesan, mozzarella, and torn basil leaves.

ALOHA PINEAPPLE CHICKEN

Here's a chicken baste that makes the bird taste like it was marinated for hours, using common ingredients most folks have on hand!

Serves: 8

Ingredients

2 whole frying chickens (about 3 pounds each)*

Aloha Pineapple Sauce:

8 ounces pineapple juice

½ cup packed dark brown sugar

⅓ cup soy sauce

3 large garlic cloves, crushed

1 tablespoon mirin or white wine**

*Pre-cut chicken parts may be substituted, but they should be from smaller chickens as large parts take too long to cook on the grill.

**Mirin is best to use here, but if you can't find it in your store—it'd be in the Asian food section and a major brand is Kikkoman—then white wine will do.

Instructions

1. Cut up chicken into serving pieces. I cut the chickens into quarters, and then cut the wings off the breast, for a total of 6 pieces.

2. Combine all sauce ingredients in a small saucepan.

3. Bring to boil and reduce heat to a simmer, and simmer, uncovered, for about 10 to 15 minutes, or until sauce is reduced by 50 percent and has a consistency like maple syrup.

4. Cool to lukewarm, then refrigerate until chilled. I recommend you make the sauce either very early in the day or the day before.

5. Preheat grill to low/medium-low heat. If you have a thermometer installed in the lid, grill temp should be 300 to 350°F.

6. Place chicken bone side down on grill, close lid and cook for 20 to 25 minutes; turn chicken and cook for an additional 20 minutes.

7. Turn up grill heat to medium-high heat.

8. Baste both sides of chicken with the sauce, and cook about 5 minutes on each side to crisp chicken.

Note: Internal temperature of chicken should be 180°F for food safety, or juices should run clear.

APRICOT CHICKEN

Tangy and absolutely delicious! You'll probably have to buy fresh apricots, but the rest you likely have on hand.

Serves: 4

Ingredients

2 pounds chicken thighs and/or drumsticks

1 pound fresh apricots, halved and pitted*

Sauce:

½ cup ketchup

1 cup apricot preserves*

1 cup brown sugar

¼ cup soy sauce

2 tablespoons white wine

1 clove garlic, minced

*Peach preserves and peaches may be substituted

Instructions

1. Preheat oven to 350°F.

2. Mix all sauce ingredients in a small saucepan and heat, stirring occasionally, until sugar and preserves are dissolved. Remove from heat and cool to room temperature.

3. Place chicken parts, skin side down, in an oven-proof 9 x 13-inch baking dish. Pour sauce over chicken, lifting chicken parts so sauce can get under them.

4. Bake for 45 minutes. Turn skin side up and bake for 35 minutes.

5. Add apricot halves and bake for an additional 10 to 15 minutes.

ASIAN CHICKEN THIGHS

This chicken dinner proves that you can get bold and wonderful flavors from quite humble ingredients. The chicken infuses with flavor as it cooks.

Serves: 4–6

Ingredients

¼ cup brown sugar

¼ cup soy sauce

½ teaspoon dark sesame oil

½ teaspoon ginger powder

1 tablespoon rice vinegar (white is OK too)

1½ pounds bone-in chicken thighs (skinless is fine)

1 tablespoon olive oil

Instructions

1. Preheat oven to 375°F.

2. Mix the brown sugar, soy sauce, sesame oil, ginger, and rice vinegar in a small bowl. Stir until sugar is dissolved. Set aside.

3. Heat a large skillet over medium-high heat. Brush top and skin side of chicken with the 1 tablespoon oil.

4. Place chicken, skin and top side down in heated skillet. Brown for 3 to 5 minutes, or until chicken releases freely from the pan. Turn and brown on other side. Remove to plate; drain fat from skillet and wipe with a paper towel.

5. Place chicken back in skillet, skin and top side up. Pour soy sauce mixture over chicken.

6. Bake for 25 to 30 minutes, or until internal temperature of chicken is 170°F and/or juices run clear.

CHICKEN CORDON BLEU CASSEROLE

If you don't want to fuss with the real thing, here's a deconstructed version of the famous chicken dish. Goes together 1-2-3 and tastes every bit as good.

Serves: 4

Ingredients

¾ cup water

¼ cup (½ stick) butter

2½ cups poultry stuffing (like Pepperidge Farm)

1 can (10.75 ounces) cream of chicken soup

1 tablespoon Dijon mustard

3 cups fresh broccoli florets

1 pound boneless skinless chicken breast, cut in bite-size pieces

6 slices deli ham, cut up

6 slices Swiss cheese

Instructions

1. Preheat oven to 375°F. Lightly grease an 7 x 11-inch baking dish.

2. In a saucepan, boil the ¾ cup water; add the butter and let it melt. Stir in the stuffing mix. Toss to coat with the butter-water mixture. Set aside.

3. In a large bowl, combine soup and Dijon mustard. Add the broccoli, chicken, and ham. Stir to coat with soup mixture.

4. Turn into prepared baking dish. Lay cheese across the top, then cover with the stuffing mix.

5. Bake for 35 to 40 minutes, or until heated through.

6. Let stand 5 to 10 minutes before serving.

CHICKEN CRESCENT BAKE

Some leftover chicken and a few ordinary ingredients is all you need to make this comforting and delicious family-style casserole.

Serves: 4

Ingredients

2 cups shredded cooked chicken

4 ounces softened cream cheese

1 teaspoon dehydrated onion minces

¼ teaspoon garlic powder

½ teaspoon salt

Pinch of pepper

1 cup shredded mozzarella cheese

1 tube (8 count) regular-size crescent rolls

¼ cup grated Parmesan or Romano cheese

Sauce:

1 can (10.75-ounce) cream of chicken soup*

1 soup can of milk (use the empty soup can)

*Cream of Mushroom may be substituted

Instructions

1. Preheat oven to 350°F .

2. Lightly spray a 7 x 11-inch rectangular baking dish.

3. In a medium bowl, mix together the chicken, cream cheese, onion, garlic powder, salt, pepper, and mozzarella. Set aside.

4. In another bowl, mix the soup with the milk, stirring the milk in gradually until smooth.

5. Separate the crescent dough into the 8 triangles. Place about ¼ cup of the chicken mixture on the wide base of the crescent triangle. Roll up and seal completely—you roll these like you are making crescent rolls, but also pinch the sides together so the filling is completely enclosed by the dough.

6. Place chicken-filled crescents in the pan, making 2 rows with 4 crescents in each row. Leave space on all sides for the sauce.

7. Pour sauce around the crescents, avoiding covering the dough with the sauce or they will not brown and will become soggy!

8. Sprinkle crescent tops with the grated Parmesan or Romano cheese, and bake for 30 to 35 minutes or until tops are nicely browned.

ITALIAN HERB CHICKEN WITH ROASTED VEGETABLES

A simple chicken dinner that cooks all in one pan. Who'd think ordinary lemons and some basic herbs could be elevated to the spectacular?

Serves: 4

Ingredients

6 tablespoons olive oil

2 lemons, 1 thinly sliced, 1 juiced

4 garlic cloves, minced

1 teaspoon salt

1 teaspoon oregano

1 teaspoon basil

½ teaspoon freshly ground black pepper

4 chicken breasts

¾ pounds green beans, trimmed

8 small red potatoes, quartered

2 tablespoons grated Parmesan cheese

Instructions

1. Preheat oven to 400°F.

2. Coat a large baking dish or cast-iron skillet with 1 tablespoon of the olive oil.

3. Arrange the lemon slices in a single layer in the bottom of the dish or skillet.

4. In a large bowl, combine the remaining oil, lemon juice, garlic, salt, oregano, basil and pepper; add the chicken, green beans, and potatoes and toss to coat. Pour this mix into the pan and spread around evenly.

5. Sprinkle the Parmesan cheese over the top.

6. Roast for 50 minutes or until cooked through.

ONE-PAN CHICKEN & ORZO SKILLET DINNER

When you need dinner in a dash, let this recipe come to your rescue. Use any frozen vegetables, and rice may be substituted for the orzo.

Serves: 2–4

Ingredients

2 medium boneless, skinless chicken breasts

2 tablespoons butter

1 cup orzo

2 cups water

2 pouches Swanson Flavor Boost*

2 tablespoons dehydrated onion

2 strips crisp bacon (optional), diced

2 cups broccoli florets

Seasoned Flour:

½ cup flour

1 teaspoon salt

½ teaspoon pepper

1 teaspoon garlic powder

Pinch curry powder

* You may use 2 cups of very rich chicken stock in place of the Flavor Boost. If you do, omit the water.

Instructions

1. With a mallet, pound chicken breast to about ½-inch thickness between 2 sheets of waxed paper.

2. Mix seasoned flour ingredients and dredge each chicken breast with the flour mixture.

3. In a large skillet over medium-high heat, melt the butter.

4. Brown chicken breasts well on each side—don't worry if the butter becomes brown butter, it's part of the flavoring process.

5. Remove chicken and in the same pan, add the uncooked orzo and brown in the remaining butter in the pan.

6. Add the 2 cups of water, the Flavor Boost, and dehydrated onion; stir.

7. Place browned chicken breast on top of orzo mixture; cover, reduce heat, and simmer for 15 minutes, then add the diced bacon and broccoli florets.

8. Cover and continue simmering for 10 to 15 minutes or until water is almost absorbed and broccoli is cooked to crisp-tender (don't let it overcook).

PEPPERJACK CHICKEN

Who'd think that so few simple ingredients could produce such a tasty and satisfying meal? Pepperjack gives this casserole a nice zip, but any cheese that melts well can be substituted!

Serves: 6

Ingredients

6 tablespoons butter, divided

4 boneless, skinless chicken breasts

1 cup sliced mushrooms (optional)

6–12 slices Pepperjack cheese*

1 can (10.75-ounce) cream of chicken soup

⅓ cup milk

2 cups seasoned poultry stuffing (like Pepperidge Farms)

*Use the 12 slices if you want it extra cheesy.

Instructions

1. Preheat oven to 350°F.

2. Melt 2 tablespoons of the butter and spread in a 9 x 13-inch baking pan.

3. Prepare the chicken breasts by cutting them in half lengthwise to make 2 thinner breast pieces, then lay the chicken breasts across the bottom of the pan so the entire bottom is covered.

4. Distribute mushrooms (if using) across the chicken breasts, then place the cheese slices on top of the chicken and mushrooms, covering them completely.

5. In a small bowl, mix the soup and the milk. Pour over top of the casserole, then spread out so everything is covered.

6. Melt the remaining 4 tablespoons of butter.

7. Distribute stuffing evenly across the top of the casserole; drizzle with the 4 tablespoons melted butter.

8. Bake at 350°F for 45 to 60 minutes, or until chicken is cooked through and the top of the casserole is bubbling.

SPICY OVEN-FRIED CHICKEN

Bypass those chicken coating mixes in the grocery store. Make your own at home with things right on your pantry shelf!

Serves: 6-8

Ingredients

3 cups cornflake crumbs

1 recipe seasoning mix

2 frying chickens (about 3 pounds each), cut up

Seasoning Mix:

1½ tablespoon kosher salt

2 tablespoons paprika

2 tablespoons smoked paprika

1 teaspoon garlic powder

1 tablespoon dry ground mustard

1 tablespoon thyme

2 teaspoons basil

1 teaspoon oregano

2 teaspoons ground ginger

Instructions

1. Preheat oven to 400°F.
2. Line a large baking pan (I use a large cookie sheet with sides—a jelly-roll pan) with foil, and spray with nonstick spray.
3. Mix cornflake crumbs with the Seasoning Mix and place in a plastic bag.
4. Rinse chicken and shake off excess water.
5. Place 1 or 2 pieces at a time in bag with crumbs. Shake to coat.
6. Place skin side up on pan.
7. Bake for 40 to 50 minutes (depending on size of chicken parts).

APPLE BUTTER BBQ RIBS

These succulent ribs can be prepared by three methods. No apple butter BBQ sauce? Make your own with store-bought BBQ sauce and your own apple butter.

Serves: 4

Ingredients

1 slab (about 3–4 pounds) pork baby back ribs

Rub:

½ cup brown sugar

1 tablespoon garlic powder

2 teaspoons onion powder

½ teaspoon thyme

½ teaspoon salt

¼ teaspoon pepper

⅛ teaspoon cayenne pepper (optional)

Apple Butter BBQ Sauce:

½ cup good BBQ sauce (like Sweet Baby Ray's)

¼ cup apple butter

Instructions

1. Mix rub ingredients together in a small bowl. Set aside.
2. Prepare ribs by removing membrane covering the bone (silver-skin) as this prevents the ribs from curling as they cook.
3. Rub all sides of the ribs with prepared rub. Place ribs in a large plastic bag and refrigerate overnight.

To prepare on the grill:

1. You will cook the ribs on the *unlit* side of the grill, so place a drip pan under that grill rack. Light one side, close lid and preheat until internal grill temp is 300°F. Place ribs on *unlit* side, close lid and cook for approximately 3 hours, or internal temp of ribs is 170°F.
2. Brush with BBQ sauce and transfer to *lit* side to crisp the ribs and brown the sauce.
3. Remove to a serving platter, cover with foil and let the ribs sit for 10 to 15 minutes. Cut into 2-rib portions.

To prepare in the oven:

1. Preheat oven to 300°F. Place ribs on a rack in a roasting pan. Roast for approximately 3 hours.
2. Brush with BBQ sauce and pop under the broiler for about 2 minutes each side.

To prepare in slow cooker:

1. Cut ribs in 2-rib portions to fit inside the crock. Cover and cook on high for 3 to 5 hours, or until ribs are 170°F. Remove ribs and drain off any accumulated liquid in the crock. Wipe the crock dry with paper towels.
2. Place ribs back in crock and pour desired amount of BBQ sauce over ribs—I suggest no more than ½ cup as you want the flavor of the rub to come through and not be overshadowed by the strength of the BBQ sauce. Cover and cook on high about 30 minutes, or until glazed.

BAKED GOLDEN RANCH PORK CHOPS

Ditch the store-bought coating mix and make your own from ingredients you already have handy!

Serves: 4

Ingredients

4 center-cut rib pork chops (about ½-inch thick)

¼ cup cream or half-and-half

Coating:

1 cup unflavored breadcrumbs

½ cup ranch seasoning mix

½ cup panko breadcrumbs

Instructions

1. Preheat oven to 425°F. Place a rack (I use a cooling rack for cookies—it fits perfectly in a large baking sheet/cookie sheet) in a large (approximately 15 inches) baking sheet/cookie sheet.

2. Mix all the coating ingredients in a plastic storage bag.

3. Pat chops dry with a paper towel.

4. Place cream in a large bowl. Dip each chop in the cream, shaking off excess.

5. Shake chops, one by one, in the coating mixture and place on the prepared baking sheet

6. Bake for 20 to 30 minutes, or until golden brown and cooked through.

BISCUITS & SAUSAGE GRAVY POT PIE

An old family favorite done casserole style and made easy thanks to everyday ingredients.

Serves: 4–6

Ingredients

1 roll (16-ounce) bulk sausage

3 tablespoons butter

¼ cup flour

2½ cups milk

1 teaspoon salt

½ teaspoon pepper

1 package (8 count) large refrigerated biscuits (like Grands)

Instructions

1. Brown sausage meat, breaking up lumps. Drain and set aside.

2. Prepare sausage gravy by melting butter over medium heat in a medium saucepan. Add flour (make a roux) and whisk so there are no lumps. Cook roux over medium heat about 2 minutes, stirring constantly. While whisking, add milk slowly, making sure there are no lumps. Add salt and pepper. Cook sauce until it begins to thicken. Add cooked sausage.

3. Pour sausage gravy into casserole. Place biscuits on top of the casserole; bake 25 to 30 minutes, or until top biscuits are golden brown.

   Note: I use reduced-fat biscuits. Also reduced-fat sausage or turkey sausage may be substituted

BOURBON-GLAZED PORK CHOPS

Here's an unusual combination. Each part on its own is not thrilling, but put them together and these chops sing!

Serves: 4

Ingredients

4 strips crisp-cooked bacon, diced

4 bone-in center-cut rib pork chops (about 1-inch thick)

Salt

Pepper

Garlic powder

Glaze:

⅓ cup molasses

¼ cup bourbon, or substitute apple cider

3 tablespoons Dijon mustard

Instructions

1. Preheat oven to 400°F. Line a large baking sheet with foil; set aside.

2. In a large skillet, fry bacon until crisp. Dice bacon. Reserve drippings and drain bacon on paper towels. Set aside.

3. In a small saucepan, combine the molasses, bourbon, and Dijon mustard. Bring to boil over medium-high heat. Reduce heat to medium-low and boil for about 10 minutes or until there is about ½ cup of reduced glaze.

4. Pat chops dry. Sprinkle with salt, pepper, and garlic powder. Brown pork chops in reserved bacon drippings on each side, about 8 to 10 minutes. Place browned chops on prepared baking sheet.

5. Coat each chop with about 1 tablespoon of the glaze.

6. Bake in preheated oven 10 to 15 minutes. Remove and drizzle additional glaze over chops. Top with diced bacon.

CAJUN SMOKED SAUSAGE ALFREDO

Have leftover sausage or kielbasa? Here's a great way to extend the meat you have left over! Add pasta and a kicky Cajun-flavored Alfredo and you're all set for dinner.

Serves: 4

Ingredients

1 package (1 pound) smoked sausage or kielbasa

1½ cups water

1½ cups tubular pasta (like penne or elbows)

2 cups heavy cream

½ cup frozen peas, defrosted

½ cup grated Parmesan cheese

2 teaspoons Cajun/creole seasoning

1 green onion, sliced

½ cup grape tomatoes

Instructions

1. Slice sausage in ¼-inch slices.

2. Heat a large skillet over medium-high heat. Brown sausage well. Remove from pan; set aside.

3. Return pan to heat and deglaze pan with the water. Add the pasta. Bring to a boil, cover, and reduce heat. Cook until water is absorbed by pasta (about 8 minutes).

4. Add the cream, peas, Parmesan, and Cajun seasoning to the pan; stir well. Add the browned sausage back to the pan; heat through.

5. Top with sliced green onion and grape tomatoes. Serve immediately.

FAKE LASAGNA

I can remember a time when ricotta and lasagna noodles were not readily available for purchase outside of large urban areas. This is the way everyone got around that! Maybe it's not authentic, but it's very flavorful and easy to make!

Serves: 4-6

Ingredients

6 ounces (uncooked) wide egg noodles

½ cup sour cream

1 cup cottage cheese

8 ounces softened cream cheese

2 tablespoons fresh snipped chives, or 1 tablespoon dehydrated chives

3–4 cooked Italian link sausages (hot or sweet)

1 tablespoon butter, melted

1½ cups prepared pasta sauce

½ cup shredded mozzarella

Instructions:

1. Preheat oven to 050°F.

2. Lightly spray a deep 2-quart baking dish. Cook noodles per package directions; drain and set aside.

3. Mix the sour cream, cottage cheese, cream cheese, and chives.

4. Slice the sausage into slices about ¼-inch thick.

5. Place half of the noodles in the prepared baking dish and drizzle with the melted butter, then top with the cream cheese mixture, followed by the remaining noodles.

6. Place sausage slices evenly over top of casserole.

7. Pour pasta sauce evenly across the top, spreading it out with a spoon to completely cover top of casserole.

8. Cover with aluminum foil and bake for 30 minutes, then uncover, top with shredded mozzarella, and cook for an additional 10 minutes.

PORK CHOPS WITH LEMON THYME CREAM SAUCE

These pork chops only sound fancy. They're easy and made with common ingredients. No heavy cream on hand? Use undiluted evaporated milk!

Serves: 4

Ingredients

4 tablespoons unsalted butter, divided

½ cup flour

1 teaspoon salt

½ teaspoon pepper

½ teaspoon garlic powder

4 rib or sirloin pork chops bone in (about ½-inch thick)*

Lemon Thyme Cream Sauce:

3 tablespoons fresh lemon juice

1 teaspoon grated lemon zest

1 garlic clove, minced

¼ cup white wine

½ teaspoon thyme

½ teaspoon salt

½ cup heavy cream

*Boneless chops may be substituted.

Instructions

1. Heat a heavy skillet over medium-high heat. Melt 2 tablespoons butter.

2. Mix the flour, salt, pepper, and garlic powder in a shallow bowl. Dredge pork chops in seasoned flour mixture, shaking off excess.

3. Brown pork chops well on both sides, about 5 to 8 minutes per side. Remove from pan and set aside.

4. In the same pan you browned the chops in, reduce the heat to medium and add the lemon juice, lemon zest, garlic, wine, thyme, and salt. Mix well.

5. Place pork chops back in pan, cover, reduce heat to low, and cook for 15 to 20 minutes.

6. Remove pork chops to a serving platter, cover, and keep warm in a 200°F oven while making sauce.

7. Increase the heat under the pan to medium. Blend in heavy cream and remaining butter. Let the mixture bubble and reduce by 25 percent—it should be like thin gravy.

8. Drizzle sauce over pork chops and serve immediately.

CLASSIC CHEDDAR BACON MACARONI & CHEESE

This originally meatless meal is made better by the addition of a good sharp Cheddar and a hint of bacon. Want it truly meatless? Leave out the bacon!

Serves: 4–6

Ingredients

2 cups uncooked elbow macaroni

For the sauce:

½ cup heavy cream

2 cups whole milk (I generally mix 1½ cups milk with ½ cup half-and-half)

1 cup cubed Velveeta

8 ounce shredded sharp Cheddar

½ teaspoon freshly ground black pepper

2–3 strips of crisp bacon, diced

For the topping:

1 cup soft breadcrumbs

1 tablespoon butter, melted

Instructions

1. Cook elbow macaroni as per package directions; drain and set aside.

2. In a medium saucepan, combine sauce ingredients, except for bacon. Stir constantly over medium heat until cheeses are melted. Reduce heat and stir constantly until sauce is slightly reduced (about 25 percent). Add the bacon.

3. While sauce is reducing, mix breadcrumbs with the melted butter. Set aside.

4. Preheat oven to 350°F. Spray or grease a 1.5-quart deep casserole.

5. Add macaroni and sauce to prepared baking dish. Top with buttered breadcrumbs.

6. Bake at 350°F for 20 to 30 minutes or until sauce bubbles along the edges and the crumbs are nicely browned.

PINEAPPLE CILANTRO SHRIMP

Sweet pineapple and earthy cilantro combine to make these shrimp irresistible!

Serves: 4

Ingredients

1 pound peeled, deveined large uncooked shrimp

Salt and pepper

Marinade:

¾ cup pineapple juice

3 large garlic cloves, minced

¼ cup olive oil

1 tablespoon brown sugar

¼ cup (packed) cilantro, roughly chopped

Instructions

1. Mix all marinade ingredients in a small bowl.

2. Place cleaned shrimp in a zipper storage/freezer bag, and pour marinade over shrimp; seal bag and invert bag a couple of times to coat shrimp.

3. Place in refrigerator for 30 minutes (do not marinate any longer than 40 minutes or the acid will "cook" the shrimp and make them rubbery). If using bamboo skewers, soak them in warm water for 30 minutes prior to cooking.

4. Preheat grill to high heat and begin to skewer shrimp. (If desired, otherwise use a grill basket. I prefer skewering as they are easier to turn, cook, and serve.)

5. Sprinkle with salt and pepper to taste, if desired, about 1 teaspoon salt, ½ teaspoon pepper in total—always salt immediately before cooking! You can discard the marinade, or place it in a small saucepan, boil, and reduce it for a delicious dipping sauce.

6. Cook shrimp about 5 minutes each side, or until pink (but you can still see some translucency in the middle). Do not overcook!

7. Sprinkle more roughly chopped cilantro over shrimp before serving, if desired.

8. Shrimp may also be broiled in a conventional broiler.

SHRIMP NEWBURG

Since shrimp have become affordable, most of us have it on hand in our freezers. So if you're getting company on short notice, this Newburg made with shrimp is sure to impress.

Serves: 4

Ingredients

2 egg yolks, slightly beaten

¼ cup butter

4 ounces fresh mushrooms, sliced

¼ cup red bell pepper, finely diced

½ cup green peas, partially cooked

2½ tablespoons flour

2 cups half-and-half (or whole milk—don't use fat-free or reduced fat)

3 tablespoons dry white wine or dry sherry

1 teaspoon salt

¼–½ teaspoon cayenne pepper

2 cups peeled cooked small shrimp* or diced cooked chicken

*I use raw shrimp and sauté them in ½ tablespoon butter until it turns pink.

Instructions

1. Place egg yolks in a small bowl and beat. Set aside.

2. Heat a large skillet or sauté pan over medium heat, and melt 3 tablespoons of the butter.

3. Add the mushrooms, pepper, and peas.

   NOTE: I used frozen peas and microwaved them on high for 30 seconds to partially cook. Sauté over medium heat until mushrooms begin to brown, then remove from pan and set them aside.

4. Add the remaining 1 tablespoon of butter to the pan; let it melt.

5. Stir the flour into the butter until you get a smooth, lump-free paste, and let it cook for about 1 minute (this is a roux).

6. Slowly add the half-and-half while stirring constantly. Cook until slightly thickened, then add the wine and stir.

7. Take about ½ cup of the hot cream mixture and stir it into the beaten egg yolks (this is tempering). Add the egg/cream mixture back to the pan while stirring constantly. Cook for 1 minute. Add the salt and cayenne pepper.

8. Add the mushrooms, peppers, and peas back to pan, then add the cooked shrimp or chicken. Heat through.

9. Serve in puff pastry cups or over rice.

EGG BASKETS

These are a fond memory from my childhood. My mother would make these on Sunday afternoon to put in my father's lunch box for Monday. She never made the cheese sauce—that's my addition. Great as a brunch item, and you have everything on hand to make these.

Serves: 6

Ingredients

6 eggs

Salt

Pepper

Paprika

Pastry*:

1½ cups flour

½ cup shredded Cheddar cheese

1 teaspoon salt

½ cup shortening

4–5 tablespoons cold water

Cheese Sauce:

1 cup plain Greek yogurt or sour cream

½ cup shredded Cheddar cheese or Velveeta

¼ cup cream

*If you don't want to be bothered making your own pie pastry, you can use the refrigerated kind. You will need enough for a double-crust pie (2 portions), however, some re-rolling will be involved, and you can just press some shredded cheese on top of each crust before cutting.

Instructions:

1. Preheat oven to 450°F.

2. Mix the flour, cheese, and salt in a medium bowl. Cut shortening into mixture until it resembles small peas. Add the water, 1 tablespoon at a time, until dough holds together. Turn dough out on a floured surface and roll out to about ⅛-inch thickness. Cut 6 5-inch circles (I find the lid of a large-sized yogurt container is the right size). Then cut 6 3-inch circles (I use a ring from a standard-mouth mason jar). You will have to cut and re-roll to get enough circles.

3. Gently fit each 5-inch circle into a standard 6-muffin cupcake/muffin pan, letting a little bit extend over the cup so you can seal.

4. Break an egg into each pastry-lined cup. Sprinkle with salt and pepper.

5. Now take the 3-inch circles and place them over the top of each cup. Seal well. Sprinkle the top of each egg cup with a bit of paprika.

6. Bake for 20 to 25 minutes.

7. Prepare cheese sauce by adding the yogurt/sour cream and cheese/Velveeta (I recommend Velveeta as sauce will not separate) to a microwave-safe bowl. Microwave on high for 30-second intervals until cheese is melted. Thin down to desired consistency with cream (add a little at a time, the amount of cream is only a guide).

LINGUINE WITH TOASTED PECAN ARUGULA PESTO

Looking for a different pesto pasta? Try this one. The pesto is made from arugula and tastes fantastic.

Serves: 4

Ingredients

8 ounces linguine, uncooked

¼ cup finely chopped toasted pecans

Pesto:

1 large garlic clove

½ teaspoon kosher salt

5 ounces box of baby arugula

¼ cup Parmesan cheese

¼ cup plus 1 tablespoon olive oil

⅛ teaspoon pepper

¼ cup toasted pecans

Instructions:

1. Make the pesto. First, mash the garlic with the salt to form a paste—use a mortar and pestle or the side of a wide, heavy knife. Then place the arugula, cheese, olive oil, pepper, mashed garlic, and toasted pecans in a food processor and process for about 1 minute.

2. Cook linguine as per package directions. Reserve about ½ cup of the pasta water before draining.

3. Toss the hot pasta with the entire amount of the arugula pesto. Add only enough of the reserved pasta water so that the mixture is not dry—the amount you add will vary as to what consistency pleases your taste.

4. Top with the chopped pecans.

QUINOA-STUFFED PEPPERS

I don't think there are too many people who don't have a box of quinoa on the shelf since this grain has become the latest craze. And most of us have a jar of salsa lurking somewhere! Here's a vegetarian-stuffed pepper that tastes so great, you won't miss the meat!

Serves: 4–6

Ingredients

1 cup quinoa (uncooked)

2 cups water (divided)

4 large or 6 medium sweet bell peppers

2 tablespoons butter

½ pound fresh mushrooms, sliced

1 medium onion, diced

1 can (28-ounce) diced tomatoes (reserve juice)

2 garlic cloves, crushed

1 jar (12-ounce) salsa

2 tablespoons dry sherry

10 ounces mozzarella, shredded (reserve a bit for the top)

Instructions

1. Preheat oven to 325°F. You will need either a 9 x 13 or 7 x 11-inch baking pan (or any that will fit the peppers and the remaining quinoa mixture).

2. Cook quinoa according to package directions, using 1 cup uncooked quinoa in 1½ cups water. Quinoa cooks like rice. I use my rice cooker for this.

3. Cut off and reserve the tops of the bell peppers. Hollow them out then steam both the tops and the peppers in the remaining ½ cup of water until slightly soft but not limp; drain and cool slightly. In a large skillet or sauté pan, melt the butter over medium heat. Add the mushrooms and onion and sauté until tender.

4. Drain the can of diced tomatoes, but reserve the juice. Add the drained tomatoes, garlic, and salsa to the onion-mushroom mixture. Stir well and simmer uncovered for 10 minutes. Then add the sherry and stir well.

5. Fold in the cooked quinoa and the mozzarella cheese.

6. Stuff peppers with the quinoa mixture—you will use about half of the mixture to stuff the peppers. Then, place stuffed peppers upright in a baking dish and sprinkle tops of each pepper with reserved cheese.

7. Stir the reserved juice from the can of tomatoes into the remaining half of the quinoa mixture and pour around peppers in the baking pan. Bake uncovered for 20 to 25 minutes.

8. Top with reserved pepper tops and bake an additional 10 to 15 minutes.

PASTA WITH MUSHROOMS & BASIL

A hearty meatless meal that uses common ingredients and doesn't leave you hungry. This is filling. Don't have Asiago? Use Romano or Parmesan cheese.

Serves: 2

Ingredients

8 ounces spaghetti

1 tablespoon unsalted butter

¼ cup olive oil

2 large garlic cloves, minced

2 cups mushrooms, quartered

2 tablespoons fresh basil, chiffonade (shredded)

1–2 ounces Asiago, thickly shredded

Instructions

1. Cook spaghetti as per package directions. Drain and set aside.

2. Heat a large skillet over medium heat. Add the butter and the olive oil. When butter is melted and begins to bubble, add the garlic and mushrooms. Sauté, stirring frequently, until mushrooms begin to sear. Remove from heat.

3. Add cooked pasta and basil to the skillet and toss to coat.

4. Top with Asiago cheese. Serve immediately.

CLEAN-THE-FRIDGE QUICHE

Don't chuck those leftover bits and pieces. Combine them to make this tasty dinner quiche.

Serves: 6–8

Ingredients

1 unbaked piecrust

4 eggs

1 cup milk or half-and-half

Salt and pepper

1 cup shredded cheese

Any fillings you like

Instructions

1. Fit piecrust into a 10-inch quiche or tart pan (if using frozen pie shell, eliminate this step), pressing up the sides.

2. Beat 4 eggs and add milk. Beat well and add salt and pepper to taste—usually ¼ teaspoon pepper and 1 teaspoon salt.

3. Add any variety of shredded cheese. I used classic Swiss in this as I had a block already open. Set aside.

4. Spread the fillings of your choice over the bottom of the pastry shell. I used a bag of wilted baby spinach, some sliced mushrooms, bacon, and ham.

5. Pour custard-cheese mixture over top. Sprinkle with Parmesan cheese, if desired.

6. Bake at 350°F for 35 to 40 minutes, or until knife inserted near center comes out clean.

7. Remove from oven and let stand for 5 minutes before slicing and serving.

EASY-PEASY SOUPS & SIDES

ACORN SQUASH CUPS

Everyone's favorite fall squash! Two on-hand ingredients take this dish from plain to wow!

Serves: 4

Ingredients

2 medium acorn squash

2 tablespoons vegan or regular butter

4 tablespoons brown sugar

Instructions

1. Cut squashes in half, lengthwise through the stem. Scoop out seeds.

2. Preheat oven to 350°F. Place about 1 inch of water in a large baking pan. Place squash halves, cut side up, in pan.

3. Fill the seed cavity of each squash half with ½ tablespoon of butter and 1 tablespoon brown sugar.

4. Bake, uncovered, for about 1 hour, or until squash is fork tender. Brush entire edible portion with syrup that formed in the seed cavity.

5. Serve immediately.

BEER BATTER ONION RINGS

Don't throw away flat beer! It has so many uses; this is but one of them!

Serves: 4

Ingredients

2 large sweet onions (Spanish, Vidalia)

2 cups buttermilk or sour milk*

Oil for frying

½ cup flour

Batter:

2 cups flour

2 teaspoons seasoned salt

10–12 ounces beer

*Milk can be soured by adding 1 tablespoon of vinegar or lemon juice to each cup of milk you use—in this case 2 tablespoons to 2 cups.

Instructions

1. Peel and slice onions into ½-inch slices.

2. Pour buttermilk into a zipper storage bag; add onion slices. Seal and marinate for a minimum of 30 minutes, or up to 1 hour.

3. Heat about 2 inches of oil in a deep skillet or sauté pan to 350°F.

4. Remove onion slices from bag; drain and separate into individual rings.

5. Mix batter ingredients, starting out using 10 ounces of beer. Add more if necessary to form a thick-but-pourable-consistency batter. Let stand 5 minutes, then shake any excess buttermilk off the onions and dredge in the ½ cup flour.

6. Dip onions back in batter, making sure it is covered completely; let excess batter drain back into bowl after coating each ring. Dip only enough rings that you can fry at a time—don't crowd the pan. It's better to fry in small batches and keep the cooked ones hot in a 200°F oven.

7. Fry about 10 to 15 minutes, turning rings halfway through the frying time, then remove from oil with tongs to plate lined with paper towels.

8. Keep warm in a 200°F oven while frying other batches.

9. Serve with Comeback Sauce on the following page.

COMEBACK SAUCE

The most versatile substance on the planet! It's a dipping sauce, salad dressing, sandwich spread, and anything else you want to make it!

Serves: 4

Ingredients

1 cup mayonnaise

¼ cup ketchup

¼ cup chili sauce (i.e. Heinz, not Thai variety)

1 teaspoon onion powder

½ teaspoon garlic powder

2 teaspoons Worcestershire sauce

1 teaspoon Creole Seasoning Blend

1 tablespoon cider vinegar

1 teaspoon pepper

¼ teaspoon hot sauce

Instructions

1. Mix all ingredients.

2. Pour into containers, cover and refrigerate at least 2 hours for flavors to blend.

CREOLE SEASONING BLEND

Don't buy pre-mixed—you have all the ingredients you need in your pantry. Makes an excellent BBQ rub!

Serves: 1 cup (approximately)

Ingredients

- 2 tablespoons onion powder
- 2 tablespoons garlic powder
- 2 tablespoons dried oregano
- 2 tablespoons dried basil
- 1½ tablespoons dried thyme
- 1 tablespoon black pepper
- 1 tablespoon white pepper
- 2½ teaspoons cayenne pepper
- 3 tablespoons paprika
- 2 tablespoons smoked paprika
- 3 tablespoons kosher salt

Instructions

1. Mix all ingredients together and store in an airtight container.

CARROT & RAISIN SALAD

Did you know this classic, old-fashioned deli treat is made from things you already have?

Serves: 6–8

Ingredients

4 cups matchstick or shredded carrots

1 cup raisins

Dressing:

¼ cup mayonnaise

2 tablespoons sugar

3 tablespoons milk or cream

Instructions

1. In a large bowl, combine the carrots and raisins. In a small bowl, mix together all dressing ingredients.

2. Pour dressing over carrots/raisins and toss to coat.

ASIAN SPINACH

Oil and garlic are all you need to make this Asian delight.

Serves: 4

Ingredients

1 tablespoon olive oil

2 garlic cloves, crushed

1 bag (about 4–5 cups) baby spinach or regular spinach, washed and de-stemmed

½–1 teaspoon coarse sea salt

Instructions

1. Heat oil and crushed garlic over high heat in large saucepan. Oil must be heated almost to the smoke point.

2. Swirl pan constantly, and remove and discard garlic when it starts to turn golden.

3. Place spinach in hot oil and stir constantly, maybe for 1 minute.

4. Add salt and stir. Spinach will wilt down to ½ the original amount.

5. Serve immediately.

CHEESY BROCCOLI RICE CASSEROLE

This versatile casserole can be a side dish or a complete meal! Leftovers and shelf items are all it takes.

Serves: 4

Ingredients

10 ounces frozen broccoli florets, defrosted and drained

1 can (10.75-ounces) cream of chicken soup

½ cup evaporated milk or cream

2 tablespoons butter

½ cup cubed Velveeta*

2 cups cooked rice

1½ cups shredded Cheddar cheese

½ teaspoon salt

½ teaspoon pepper

2 cups cooked cubed chicken (optional)

Topping:

1 cup Ritz cracker crumbs

2 tablespoons butter, melted

*The Velveeta may be omitted. I add this as Velveeta stops any cheese sauce from separating and keeps it creamy. I happen to like it too, but if you don't, just leave it out.

Instructions

1. Preheat oven to 350°F. Lightly spray a 1.5-quart ovenproof baking dish.

2. Cut broccoli florets into pieces all about the same size.

3. In a large microwave-safe bowl, combine soup, evaporated milk, butter, and Velveeta. Microwave on high for about 1 minute; remove and stir. If mixture still has large chunks of the Velveeta, then microwave an additional 30 seconds. Remove and stir until almost smooth.

4. Add cooked rice, broccoli, shredded Cheddar, salt, pepper, and chicken, if using, to bowl with the soup/cheese mixture. Mix well.

5. Turn into prepared baking dish.

6. Mix Ritz crumbs with melted butter, so all crumbs are coated. Top casserole with buttered crumbs.

7. Bake 30 to 35 minutes, or until crumbs are browned and sauce bubbles on the edges of the baking dish.

CLASSIC MACARONI SALAD

You have everything you need to make this timeless classic right in your pantry and refrigerator.

Serves: 6–8

Ingredients

2 cups elbow macaroni (uncooked)

2 stalks celery, finely diced

¼ cup red onion, finely diced

½ cup carrots, julienne (matchstick)

Dressing:

1¼ cups mayonnaise

2 tablespoons yellow mustard

1 teaspoon salt

¼ teaspoon garlic powder

Instructions

1. Cook macaroni per package directions.

2. Drain and rinse; place in a large bowl and set aside until cool.

3. Add the celery, red onion, and carrots to the cooked macaroni; mix well.

4. In a small bowl, mix all the dressing ingredients.

5. Add dressing to macaroni and gently mix to coat all the pasta.

6. Cover and refrigerate for about 1 hour.

CREAM OF BROCCOLI CHEDDAR SOUP

One of the greatest classic cream soups ever! This side can double as a main course—a crusty roll and a salad on the side is all it takes.

Serves: 6

Ingredients

4 tablespoons unsalted butter

¼ cup celery, finely chopped

¼ cup onion, finely chopped

⅛ teaspoon thyme

2 teaspoons salt

1 teaspoon pepper

2 chicken stock cubes

1 package (10-ounce) frozen chopped broccoli, thawed

3½ cups water

½ cup cornstarch

1½ cups heavy cream

2 cups shredded sharp Cheddar cheese

1 cup milk, for thinning the soup, if desired

Instructions

1. Melt butter over medium heat in a large saucepan or Dutch oven. Add the celery, onion, thyme, salt, and pepper. Sauté until onion is tender—about 5 minutes.

2. Add the stock cubes, broccoli, and 3 cups of water. Bring to boil, cover, and reduce heat to low. Simmer 15 minutes.

3. Mix the cornstarch and the ½ cup water. This is a *lot* of cornstarch, but you want it to become the consistency of a pudding so you must use a lot. Stir in the cornstarch and when bubbles begin to rise to the surface, slowly add the heavy cream, blending well. Stirring constantly, add the shredded cheese and stir until melted.

4. If the consistency is too thick for you taste, you can thin to the desired consistency using the milk. Use just enough milk to get it to the consistency you prefer. I use about ¼ cup of milk, but the amount may vary depending on your preference.

5. Serve immediately (as thickened products that use a cornstarch base will break down quickly).

CORN RELISH

Make this one up fresh and it's a salad. Process it in a water bath and it becomes a relish! We used to call that relish "chow chow" but how accurate that is we don't know. But we do know it's delicious!

Serves: 6

Ingredients

4 cups cooked corn

¾ cup red bell pepper, diced

¾ cup green bell pepper, diced

½ cup white onion, chopped

Brine/Dressing:

2 cups white vinegar

⅔ cup sugar

1 tablespoon kosher salt

1 teaspoon celery seed

1 tablespoon mustard seed

1 teaspoon ground turmeric

Instructions

1. In a nonreactive saucepan (stainless steel, ceramic coated), heat the brine/dressing ingredients to dissolve the sugar.

2. Remove from heat and cool.

3. Mix remaining ingredients in a large bowl and pour cooled brine/dressing over corn mixture.

4. Toss and chill for about 1 hour.

CUCUMBER DILL SALAD

This deli staple is easily made at home with things that are already in your crisper and pantry.

Serves: 8

Ingredients

1 seedless cucumber
1 medium white onion

Brine:
1 teaspoon dill
½ cup white vinegar
2 cups water
1 tablespoon kosher salt
¼ teaspoon pepper
¼ cup sugar

Instructions

1. Using a mandoline (preferred) or a knife, cut cucumber into very thin slices.

2. Slice onion slightly thicker—maybe ¹⁄₁₆-inch thicker. Cut round onion slices in half and separate.

3. Mix brine ingredients, stirring until sugar and salt are dissolved.

4. Place cucumbers and onions in a nonreactive (ceramic, glass, or stainless steel) large bowl.

5. Pour brine over cucumber mixture and stir to make sure it is immersed in the brine.

6. Cover and refrigerate at least 24 hours.

FIESTA RICE SALAD WITH HOUSE SPECIAL DRESSING

What a great way to use leftover rice and bits and bobs from the crisper! The dressing can also be used as a creamy salad dressing. Nothing exotic here, and requires standard shelf items.

Serves: 8

Ingredients

Salad:

4 cups cooked cold rice

½ cup celery, diced

¼ cup red onion, diced

½ cup carrots, shredded

½ cup cooked bacon, diced

1 cup grape tomatoes, cut in half

2 tablespoons fresh chives, snipped (optional)

House Special Dressing:

1 cup mayonnaise

1 package Good Seasons Italian dressing mix

⅓ cup white wine vinegar

2 tablespoons olive oil

1 tablespoon sugar

1 tablespoon parsley

¼ cup Parmesan Romano mixture

1 tablespoon water

½ teaspoon garlic powder

Instructions

1. Mix all salad ingredients in a large bowl. Cover and refrigerate until ready to serve.

2. Mix all dressing ingredients in a small bowl. Chill for at least 2 hours.

3. Mix desired amount of dressing into salad. Serve immediately.

GARLIC ASIAGO FINGERLING POTATOES

While fingerling potatoes may not be in your pantry, we bet that regular potatoes are, and they can be easily substituted in this tasty side dish.

Serves: 4–6

Ingredients

2 pounds fingerling potatoes, cut in half lengthwise

2 teaspoons salt

1 teaspoon garlic powder

1 teaspoon oregano

½ teaspoon basil

¼ teaspoon pepper

⅛ teaspoon hot red pepper flakes (optional)

¼ cup olive oil

¼ cup shredded Asiago cheese

2 tablespoons fresh snipped chives or parsley

Instructions

1. Dry cut side of potatoes with a paper towel.

2. Line a large baking sheet with parchment or spray with non-stick spray.

3. Mix the salt, garlic powder, oregano, basil, pepper, and hot pepper flakes in a small bowl.

4. Preheat oven to 375°F.

5. Place potatoes in a large bowl and add the olive oil. Toss to coat well.

6. Lay potatoes, skin side down, on prepared baking sheet and sprinkle salt mixture and shredded Asiago evenly over tops of potatoes.

7. Bake for 30 to 40 minutes, or until potatoes are tender and cheese begins to brown.

8. Garnish with the chives or parsley.

GERMAN POTATO SALAD

Now you can duplicate the deli right in your own kitchen! This timeless warm salad uses everyday ingredients you already have on hand.

Serves: 6

Ingredients

1½ pounds small red potatoes

1 teaspoon salt, plus more for boiling potatoes

4 slices bacon

¾ cup water

¼ cup plus 2 tablespoons cider vinegar

2 tablespoons sugar

½ teaspoon celery seed

¼ teaspoon pepper

1 small onion, chopped

2 tablespoons flour

Instructions

1. Scrub potatoes well. Place in a large saucepan with enough water to cover them. Add the salt, bring to boil, reduce heat; cover and cook for approximately 25 to 30 minutes or until potatoes are tender, then drain water and let cool until they can be handled.

2. When potatoes are cool enough to handle, slice them in ¼-inch (approximate) slices, leaving skin on. Set aside.

3. Slice bacon into 1-inch pieces.

4. Mix the water, vinegar, sugar, salt, pepper, and celery seed in a small bowl. Set aside.

5. In a large (10 to 12-inch) skillet, cook bacon pieces until crisp. Remove from pan with slotted spoon and drain on paper towels.

6. Add the chopped onion to the bacon drippings and sauté over medium heat until the onion is translucent, then add the flour, stirring until no lumps remain.

7. Slowly add the vinegar mixture to the pan, stirring constantly; bring to boil and stir for 1 minute.

8. Add the potato slices and bacon to the skillet, gently stirring/tossing to coat potatoes with dressing.

9. Can be served warm from the pan or chilled.

KICKED-UP COLESLAW

Old Bay Seasoning takes ordinary to fantastic with this coleslaw.

Serves: 6–8

Ingredients

- 5–6 cups shredded cabbage
- ¼ cup carrot, grated
- 1 cup mayonnaise
- 1 tablespoon water
- 2 tablespoons cider vinegar
- 1 tablespoon garlic powder
- 2 tablespoons sugar
- ½ teaspoon kosher salt
- 1 teaspoon Old Bay Seasoning
- ¼ teaspoon black pepper

Instructions

1. Place shredded cabbage and carrots in a large bowl.

2. Mix remaining ingredients in a small bowl. Pour over cabbage and mix well to coat. Coleslaw may appear dry, but water will release as it sets (pickles).

3. Cover and refrigerate for at least 2 hours. The longer it sits, the more it pickles, and there will be plenty of juice.

PASTA AND GREEN BEAN SALAD WITH LEMON TARRAGON DRESSING

Substitute blanched frozen whole beans for fresh here. Even canned cut beans will do in a pinch!

Serves: 4–6

Ingredients

8 ounces medium shells pasta (uncooked)

1 pound fresh green beans

¼ cup grated Parmesan cheese

Salt and pepper to taste

¼ cup sliced almonds, toasted

Dressing:

1 teaspoon grated lemon zest

1 medium lemon, juiced

1 tablespoon sugar

1 teaspoon dried tarragon leaves

2 tablespoons water

⅓ cup olive oil

Instructions

1. Cook shells per package directions; drain and let cool.

2. Remove stems and strings from green beans. Cut them in half, then steam or microwave for 2 minutes.

3. Place immediately in ice water and let stand 5 minutes; drain.

4. Mix all dressing ingredients in a blender or food processor, then place in a covered container and refrigerate for about 2 hours.

5. In a large bowl, mix pasta, green beans, Parmesan cheese, salt, and pepper.

6. Chill about 2 hours.

7. When ready to serve, add desired amount of dressing and toss to coat.

8. Top with toasted almonds.

ROASTED MAPLE BRUSSELS SPROUTS

Just two ingredients, but tons of flavor. This recipe actually turned a confirmed hater into a Brussels sprouts lover!

Serves: 4

Ingredients

1 pound fresh Brussels sprouts

2 tablespoons olive oil

1 teaspoon salt

¼ teaspoon pepper

3 tablespoons maple syrup

Instructions

1. Preheat oven to 350°F. Line a baking sheet with foil or parchment paper.

2. Wash sprouts. Cut stems off sprout bottoms, then cut into quarters through stem. Place in a large bowl and toss with oil, salt, and pepper.

3. Lay sprouts in a single layer on prepared baking sheet. Drizzle with maple syrup.

4. Bake for 20 to 30 minutes, turning halfway during cook time.

TOASTED ISRAELI COUSCOUS WITH MUSHROOMS

Israeli, or pearl, couscous maybe isn't in your pantry—but it should be!
So many delicious sides, and even main dishes can be made with it!

Serves: 4

Ingredients

1 tablespoon olive oil

2 tablespoons minced onion

¼ cup butter, divided

2 cups sliced assorted gourmet mushrooms*

2 cups Israeli (pearl) couscous (I use Bob's Red Mill)

2½ cups water

1 stock cube (chicken or vegetable)

Salt and pepper to taste

¼ cup fresh chives, chopped

Pinch of thyme

*I use a combination of baby bellas, shiitake, and crimini mushrooms.

Instructions

1. In a large, heavy skillet or sauté pan, heat olive oil over medium-high heat until oil shimmers. Add onion and sauté for about 1 minute, then add 2 tablespoons of butter.

2. When butter melts, add the mushrooms and sauté until they begin to brown.

3. Add 2 more tablespoons of the butter; melt.

4. Add the couscous and stir until couscous is toasted, about 3 to 5 minutes, then add the stock cube and 1 cup of water.

5. Stir until water is almost absorbed. Repeat with second cup of water.

6. Add salt and pepper to taste at this point, along with the pinch of thyme and remaining ½ cup of water.

7. Add the remaining butter when water is almost absorbed.

8. Serve topped with chopped fresh chives.

SCALLOPED POTATOES GRATIN

Perfect potatoes! Change the cheeses for what you have on hand and you're set. The only requirement is the cheeses you use have to be ones that melt well.

Serves: 6

Ingredients

3 tablespoons butter plus extra for greasing the pan

1 garlic clove, cut in half

1 teaspoon salt

½ teaspoon pepper

6 medium potatoes, peeled and sliced about 1/16-inch thick (use a mandoline, seriously)

Sauce:

1 cup rich chicken stock

1½ cups heavy cream

3 tablespoons flour

1 cup Gouda, shredded (don't use smoked Gouda as it doesn't melt well), or Fontina cheese

1 cup grated Parmesan cheese

Salt and pepper to taste for the sauce

Instructions

1. Preheat oven to 375°F.
2. Grease a 2 to 2½–quart baking dish and rub the cut side of the garlic around the interior of the pan; discard garlic. Mix the salt and pepper.
3. Layer the potatoes in the pan, sprinkling with the salt and pepper between layers.

Sauce:

1. Melt 3 tablespoons butter in a large saucepan over medium-low heat.
2. Mix the chicken stock and cream together in a large measuring cup or bowl; set aside.
3. Carefully mix the flour into the melted butter—you want a smooth paste. Let the roux bubble around the sides of the pan.
4. Slowly add the cream-stock mixture, stirring constantly. Bring to a boil, reduce heat and simmer for 3 to 5 minutes.
5. Remove the saucepan from the heat and add the shredded Gouda; stir until cheese is melted. Season with salt and pepper.
6. Pour sauce over sliced potatoes in pan. Top with the grated Parmesan cheese and bake at 375°F for 45 to 60 minutes.
7. Remove from oven. Let the casserole stand 5 to 10 minutes before serving.

BEST NO-FUSS BREADS & MUFFINS

BACON CHEESE PULL-APARTS

Who doesn't have a can of refrigerated biscuits (often called "wampum" biscuits because you wamp 'um on the edge of a table to open them) in the fridge? Serve these up as either a side dish or an appetizer and watch them disappear . . . fast!

Serves: 6

Ingredients

1 can (8 count) large flaky biscuits (like Grands)

1 egg

2 tablespoons milk

1 teaspoon hot sauce

¾ cup Cheddar cheese

4 green onions, finely sliced

5 slices crisp bacon, diced

Instructions

1. Preheat oven to 350°F. Spray an 7 x 11-inch pan with nonstick spray.

2. Separate biscuits and cut each biscuit into quarters.

3. Beat egg and milk thoroughly; beat in hot sauce. Add biscuit quarters to milk mixture and stir gently, coating all sides of the biscuits.

4. Stir in cheese, green onions, and bacon.

5. Turn onto prepared pan, making sure biscuits are arranged in a single layer.

6. Bake at 350°F for 20 to 30 minutes, or until golden brown and cheese starts to brown.

CHEESY ONION MONKEY BREAD

This is a real crowd pleaser! Made with common ingredients, this one is even good the next day if there are any leftovers.

Serves: 6–8

Ingredients

2 containers large buttermilk biscuits (like Grands)

1½ cups shredded mozzarella cheese

1½ cups shredded sharp Cheddar cheese

½ cup green onions, chopped

6 tablespoons butter, melted

Instructions

1. Preheat oven to 350°F.

2. Spray or lightly grease a 10-cup tube or Bundt pan. This isn't necessary for a nonstick pan. Separate biscuits.

3. Cut each biscuit into quarters and place in a large bowl.

4. Add cheeses and onions, stirring to distribute evenly.

5. Melt butter and pour over biscuit mixture in bowl, stirring to coat biscuits with the butter.

6. Turn into prepared pan, distributing the biscuit mixture evenly.

7. Lightly press biscuits down.

8. Bake at 350°F for 30 to 35 minutes, or until biscuits are done and golden brown. Good served warm or cold.

AMISH WHITE BREAD

The very best and easiest bread you'll ever make, and you just won't believe it could come from what everyone has on hand!

Makes: 1 loaf

Ingredients

1 cup warm water (110°F)

⅓ cup sugar

2¼ teaspoons active dry yeast, or 2 teaspoons SAF yeast*

¾ teaspoon salt

2 tablespoons vegetable oil, plus more for bowl

3 cups flour (all-purpose or bread flour is fine)

*SAF yeast is often called "Bread Machine Yeast" or "Instant Yeast."

Instructions

1. In a large bowl, combine the warm water, sugar, and yeast. Stir and let stand for about 10 minutes—this is "proofing" the yeast. If you get a bubbly foam on the top of the water, your yeast is active and you may proceed.

2. Add the salt and vegetable oil. Stir to combine.

3. Add the flour, one cup at a time until a soft dough forms. You may have to use more flour depending on weather conditions. For instance, when I last baked this bread, I needed close to 3¾ cups of all-purpose to get this right. The dough should be soft but not sticky.

4. Turn dough out onto a floured surface and knead for about 5 minutes. If using a stand mixer with a dough hook, knead for about 3 minutes.

5. Pour some oil (about 1 teaspoon) in a large bowl and place the kneaded dough in that bowl, coating the bottom of the dough with the oil. Turn oil-side up and cover the bowl with a greased piece of plastic wrap.

6. Set the bowl in a warm, draft-free place and let rise until it doubles in bulk—between 1 to 1½ hours.

7. Punch dough down. Turn out onto lightly floured surface and shape into a loaf—this is done by pressing the dough into a sort of rectangle, then rolling up tightly from the smaller end. Seal edges and place in a 9 x 5-inch loaf pan that has been sprayed with nonstick spray. Cover with greased plastic wrap and place in a warm, draft-free place to rise until doubled in bulk—when loaf is about 1-inch higher than the side of the pan. This should take anywhere from 30 minutes to 1 hour, depending on temperature and humidity conditions.

8. Heat oven to 350°F. Bake in preheated oven for 30 minutes.

9. Remove from pan and cool completely on a rack.

EASY IRISH SODA BREAD

A staple for St. Paddy's Day that can be enjoyed year round because of the simple staple ingredients.

Makes: 2 round loaves

Ingredients

- 1 cup currants, raisins, or dried cranberries
- 4 cups bread flour
- 1 tablespoon baking powder
- ¾ teaspoon baking soda
- 1 teaspoon salt
- ½–1 tablespoon caraway seeds (optional)
- 2 cups buttermilk

Instructions

1. Preheat oven to 350°F.
2. Line a large baking sheet with parchment or lightly grease. Set aside.
3. Rinse whatever dried fruit you are using in a strainer under hot water, and place on paper towel to absorb excess water.
4. In the bowl of a heavy-duty stand mixer fitted with dough hook, add the flour, baking powder, baking soda, and salt; mix for about 1 minute.
5. Add the fruit and caraway seeds, if using.
6. With mixer running, add the buttermilk gradually—using only enough to form a soft dough (I had to use the whole 2 cups of buttermilk).
7. Knead for 1 minute, then turn the dough out onto a well-floured surface and shape into 2 rounds and place on prepared baking sheet.
8. With a sharp knife, cut an "x" about ¼-inch deep on each loaf. Sprinkle with additional flour if desired.
9. Bake for 45 to 55 minutes, or until golden brown and a toothpick inserted in the center comes out clean.

EASY HAWAIIAN ROLLS

Why buy the expensive kind at the store when you can make this very credible copycat from ingredients you already have.

Makes: 9 rolls

Ingredients

1 cup warm water or pineapple juice

⅓ cup sugar

2¼ teaspoons instant (SAF) yeast (aka bread machine yeast)

2 tablespoons oil

¾ teaspoon salt

3 cups bread flour

Instructions

1. Place water (or pineapple juice) in a large bowl. Add the sugar and stir until dissolved. Sprinkle yeast on top and let sit for 10 minutes. If bubbles form, yeast is active and you may proceed.

2. Add the oil and salt; stir.

3. Stir in flour, one cup at a time, until a soft dough forms. Turn out onto floured surface and knead for 5 to 8 minutes or until dough is smooth and elastic.

4. Place about 1 teaspoon of oil in the bottom of a deep bowl. Add the dough and coat the bottom of the dough with the oil; turn dough oil side up. Cover and let rise for 1 to 1½ hours, or until doubled in bulk.

Stand mixer method:

1. Place water/pineapple juice in the bowl of a heavy-duty stand mixer. Add the sugar and stir. Sprinkle yeast over liquid. Let stand for 10 minutes. If bubbles form, you may proceed.

2. Attach dough hook to machine. Add the oil and the salt. Mix at low speed.

3. Add flour, one cup at a time, and knead for 3 minutes. Proceed as above.

Bread machine method:

1. Add ingredients as per manufacturer's instructions. Set on dough cycle. When time is up, proceed to "shaping" instructions.

Shaping and baking:

1. Lightly spray or grease a 9 x 9-inch pan.

2. Turn dough out onto a lightly floured surface. Roll dough into a 9-inch log. Cut off 9 equal portions and form into balls. Place in pan, allowing space around each ball for rising.

3. Cover and let rise until doubled in bulk, about 30 to 45 minutes.

4. Preheat oven to 350°F. Bake rolls for 15 to 20 minutes, or until internal temperature of rolls is 190°F, or until when bottom of the rolls are tapped, it produces a hollow sound.

5. While still hot, brush tops of each roll with butter.

HONEY WHEAT BREAD

Here is a wheat bread that is so good, you'll eat it like dessert! The texture is soft and silky—not a mealy bite in sight!

Makes: 2 loaves

Ingredients

2 envelopes active yeast (bread machine/instant yeast)

¼ cup warm water

Pinch of sugar

2½ cups very warm water (120–130°F)

½ cup honey

¼ cup butter, softened

3 teaspoons kosher salt

4½ cups whole-wheat flour

2¾–3¾ cups bread flour

1 teaspoon oil

*If your heavy-duty stand mixer has a dough hook, you may switch to that when you add the last of the whole-wheat flour. If using the dough hook to knead, knead for 5 minutes after the last addition of the bread flour.

Instructions

1. Dissolve the yeast in a large bowl of the warm water; add sugar. Let stand 10 minutes. If bubbles form, the yeast is active and you may proceed with making the bread.

2. Add to the bowl the 2½ cups very warm water, honey, butter, salt and 3½ cups of the whole-wheat flour. Mix with electric mixer until a dough forms that begins to leave the sides of the bowl*.

3. Add the remaining 1 cup of whole-wheat flour and 2½ to 2¾ cups of the bread flour. Once incorporated, turn out onto a lightly floured surface and knead in the remaining ½ to 1 cup of the bread flour. Knead for 5 to 10 minutes.

4. Put about 1 teaspoon of oil in a large bowl, then add the dough and coat the bottom of it with the oil. Turn dough oil side up and cover with greased plastic wrap.

5. Place in a warm, draft-free place to rise until doubled in bulk—about 30 to 45 minutes. I use the "oven rise" method since my house is drafty. To do this, turn on your oven and run for one minute after the heat begins to come up. Turn the oven off. This is the perfect temp for yeast dough rising. You may also put a pan of hot water under the bowl with the dough.

6. When dough is doubled in bulk, punch down and divide into 2 balls. Shape each ball into a loaf and place in a well-greased 9 x 5 x 4-inch or 8 x 4 x 3-inch loaf pans. Cover with greased plastic wrap and allow to rise until doubled in bulk in a warm, draft-free place for 30 to 45 minutes.

7. Preheat oven to 375°F. Remove plastic wrap from the pans and bake loaves for 30 minutes. Reduce oven temp to 350°F and bake for an additional 10 to 15 minutes. Loaves should sound hollow when tapped on the bottom.

8. Remove from pans immediately and cool completely on a rack.

LEMON–LIME SODA BISCUITS

Often called "7-Up" biscuits because one of the main ingredients is the famous soda pop! These are some of the best biscuits you'll ever eat. Easy too . . . and using simple ingredients.

Makes: 12 biscuits

Ingredients

4 tablespoons melted butter

3 cups baking mix (like Bisquick)

¾ cup sour cream

¾ cup lemon-lime soda or any clear, carbonated beverage

Additional flour/baking mix for kneading

Instructions

1. Preheat oven to 450°F. Pour melted butter into a 7 x 11-inch baking pan.

2. Mix the baking mix, sour cream, and add just enough soda pop to make a soft dough that you can handle.

3. Turn out onto well-floured surface and knead a few times. Pat the dough down to about ½ to ¾-inches in height.

4. Using a well-floured biscuit or cookie cutter, cut out biscuits and place in prepared pan. Try to line 3 across the short side and 4 down the long side.

5. Bake for 12 to 15 minutes, or until golden brown. I brushed the tops with some butter from the pan after about 10 minutes in the oven.

POBLANO & CHEESE CORNBREAD

Don't have poblanos? Jalapeño or any other hot pepper may be used—or plain sweet bell peppers in a pinch. This cheesy cornbread is the perfect side for a bowl of steaming chili!

Makes: 1 (9 x 13) pan

Ingredients

1 cup butter, melted

1 cup sugar

4 eggs

1 (15-ounce) can creamed corn

¼ cup poblano peppers, diced

½ cup shredded Monterey Jack cheese

½ cup shredded Cheddar cheese

1 cup flour

1 cup yellow cornmeal

4 teaspoons baking powder

¼ teaspoon salt

Instructions

1. Preheat oven to 300°F. Grease a 9 x 13 baking pan.

2. In a large bowl, beat together the butter and sugar. Beat in eggs one at a time. Blend in creamed corn, peppers, Monterey Jack, and Cheddar cheese.

3. In a separate bowl, stir together flour, cornmeal, baking powder, and salt.

4. Add flour mixture to corn mixture; stir until smooth. Pour batter into prepared pan.

6. Bake in preheated oven for 1 hour, until a toothpick inserted into center of the pan comes out clean.

SYLVIA'S CRANBERRY ORANGE BREAD

A fall and Thanksgiving tradition! Fresh cranberries may be frozen so pick some up when they're on sale around the holidays so you can make this year round.

Makes: 1 loaf

Ingredients

¼ cup butter, softened

1 cup sugar

1 egg

1 teaspoon orange zest

2 cups all-purpose flour

1 teaspoon baking powder

1 teaspoon salt

½ teaspoon baking soda

¾ cup orange juice

1 cup chopped fresh or frozen cranberries

1 cup golden raisins or walnuts (both optional)

Instructions

1. In a large bowl, cream butter and sugar.
2. Beat in egg and orange zest.
3. Combine the dry ingredients; add to creamed mixture alternately with juice.
4. Fold in cranberries and raisins or walnuts (if using).
5. Pour into a greased, parchment-lined 9 x 5-inch loaf pan.
6. Bake at 350° for 60 to 65 minutes or until a toothpick inserted near the center comes out clean.
7. Cool for 10 minutes; remove from pan to a wire rack to cool completely.

CHOCOLATE CHIP BANANA BREAD

This easy-peasy banana bread is made in a jiffy! The addition of chocolate chips make it a bit special. Leave them out if you don't have them!

Makes: 1 loaf

Ingredients

3 ripe bananas, mashed

⅓ cup melted butter

1 egg, beaten

¾ cup sugar

1 teaspoon vanilla

1 teaspoon baking soda

⅛ teaspoon salt

1½ cups flour

½ cup mini chocolate chips

Instructions

1. Preheat oven to 350°F.

2. Spray an 8 x 4-inch loaf pan with nonstick spray.

3. In a large bowl, mix the mashed bananas and melted butter.

4. Add the egg, sugar, and vanilla; combine well.

5. Sprinkle the baking soda and salt on top and stir well. Stir in the flour, mixing well, but being careful not to overmix.

6. Fold in chocolate chips.

7. Bake at 350°F for 50 to 60 minutes, or until a toothpick inserted near the center comes out clean.

CHOCOLATE CHIP MUFFINS

Chocolate chips are my favorite, but you can make these muffins with anything you like! Try blueberries or raspberries for a fruity twist!

Makes: 12 regular-size, 6 Texas-size muffins

Ingredients

½ cup butter, softened

1 cup sugar*

2 teaspoons baking powder

½ teaspoon salt

1 teaspoon vanilla

2 eggs

½ cup milk

2 cups flour

1 cup chocolate chips*

*You can reduce the sugar to ¾ cup if you don't like them overly sweet and want them more "muffin-y" rather than "cake-y." You can also use ½ cup mini chocolate chips if you want them smaller and more evenly dispersed and to cut fat and calories.

Instructions

1. Preheat oven to 350°F. Grease or line with paper cups, either a 12-count regular muffin pan or a 6-count Texas muffin pan.

2. In a large bowl, add the butter, sugar, baking powder, and salt. Beat until light and fluffy. Beat in the vanilla and eggs, beating well. Add the milk and beat until incorporated.

3. Stir in the flour and chocolate chips until well mixed. Distribute batter evenly into muffin tins.

4. Bake smaller muffins 25 to 30 minutes. Bake large Texas-style muffins 30 to 40 minutes, or until toothpick inserted in the center comes out clean.

5. Remove from oven and cool on wire racks.

STRAWBERRY SPICE MUFFINS

Fresh or frozen strawberries can be used in these unusual muffins. The spices may be left out if you prefer pure strawberry flavor.

Makes: 12 regular-size or 6 Texas-size muffins

Ingredients

2 cups flour

1 cup sugar

½ teaspoon salt

1 teaspoon baking soda

1½ teaspoons cinnamon

⅛ teaspoon nutmeg

1 cup fresh strawberries, diced

2 eggs

¾ cup milk

¼ cup oil

Topping:

¼ cup quick oats

2 tablespoons flour

3 tablespoons sugar

½ teaspoon cinnamon

1 tablespoon butter, melted

Instructions

1. Preheat oven to 350°F. Grease or line with paper cups, either a 12-count regular muffin pan or a 6-count Texas muffin pan.

2. Mix all topping ingredients. Set aside.

3. In a large bowl, combine the first 6 ingredients. Mix well. Add the diced strawberries to the dry ingredients, tossing to coat them well. This will prevent them from sinking to the bottom of the muffin.

4. Make a well in the center. In a small bowl, beat the eggs, milk, and oil. Add the milk mixture in the well of the dry ingredients. Mix only until the dry ingredients are wet. Resist the urge to overmix—it's OK if there are lumps.

5. Pour into prepared pan, filling cups ¾ full. Sprinkle topping over muffins.

6. Bake 30 to 35 minutes or until toothpick inserted in the center of muffins comes out clean.

7. Remove from oven and cool 10 minutes. Remove to rack to cool completely.

RICOTTA LEMON POPPY MUFFINS

Ricotta maybe one ingredient you don't have in the fridge, but it's worth putting on your grocery list to make these muffins. Tangy and moist, they're sure to be a hit!

Makes: 12 regular-size or 6 Texas-size muffins

Ingredients

1 box lemon, yellow, or white cake mix

1 package lemon-flavored instant pudding

4 eggs

⅓ cup vegetable oil

¼ cup poppy seeds

1 cup ricotta cheese

2 teaspoons lemon zest

Granulated sugar for topping

Instructions

1. Preheat oven to 350°F.

2. Prepare muffin pans by either lining with papers or greasing/spraying with nonstick spray.

3. Add all ingredients, except the granulated sugar, in a large bowl. With electric mixer, beat for 2 minutes—I suggest using a heavy-duty stand mixer as this batter is very dense.

4. Fill muffin cups ⅔ full, and sprinkle with granulated sugar.

5. Bake at 350°F for 20 to 25 minutes or until toothpick inserted in center comes out clean.

6. Cool in pans for 5 minutes.

7. Remove to rack to cool completely.

SWEETEST-EVER HAPPY ENDINGS

CHOCOLATE PEANUT BUTTER COOKIE DOUGH BITES

A chocolate and peanut butter lover's delight! A few shelf ingredients are all you need to make this indulgent treat!

Makes: 16 1-inch squares

Ingredients

1 pound box confectioner's sugar

½ cup cocoa powder

¼ cup unsalted butter, melted

½ cup milk or cream

½ cup shelled or cocktail peanuts

1 cup peanut butter morsels

Instructions

1. Grease an 8 x 8-inch square pan well.

2. Sift confectioner's sugar and cocoa together into a large microwave-safe bowl. Set aside.

3. Add the melted butter and the milk to the confectioner's sugar-cocoa mixture. Stir well until most of the dry ingredients are moistened.

4. Place the bowl in the microwave and heat on high for 2 minutes, until it bubbles. Stir in the peanuts until all the sugar is dissolved.

5. Pour quickly into the prepared pan, distributing evenly.

6. Sprinkle with the peanut butter morsels, lightly pressing the morsels into the chocolate mixture.

7. Cool for about 15 minutes on the counter, then refrigerate until thoroughly chilled.

FUDGE SAUCE

Always good to have a jar of this on hand for desserts and ice cream.

Serves: 2 cups (approximately)

Ingredients

⅔ cup heavy cream

½ cup light corn syrup

¼ cup Dutch-process cocoa

⅓ cup dark brown sugar

¼ teaspoon salt

6 ounces dark/semisweet/bittersweet chocolate, chopped finely and divided

2 tablespoons unsalted butter

1 teaspoon vanilla

Instructions

1. Place cream, corn syrup, cocoa, sugar, salt and 3 ounces of the chopped chocolate in a small (1 to 1.5-quart) saucepan.

2. Bring to boil over medium heat, stirring occasionally. Reduce heat to low and continue to slowly boil for 5 minutes, stirring every now and then.

3. Remove from heat.

4. Add the rest of the chocolate, butter, and vanilla and stir until chocolate and butter are melted and sauce is smooth.

5. Cool to warm and serve over ice cream, cake, etc.

6. May be stored in a tightly covered container in the refrigerator and warmed when needed.

DEATH BY CHOCOLATE
CHEESECAKE BROWNIE CUPS

Chocolate lovers are swooning over this! It requires you to use the real thing a high-percentage cacao chocolate, but this dessert is well worth the investment in the ingredients.

Makes: 12 cupcakes or 6 Revol cups

Ingredients

Brownie*:

2 cups sugar

1¼ cup flour

¼ teaspoon salt

6 tablespoons baking cocoa

4 eggs, beaten

¾ cup oil

1 teaspoon vanilla

Cheesecake Filling:

6 ounces cream cheese or Neufchatel cheese

3 tablespoons very soft butter

1 teaspoon vanilla

2 tablespoons flour

⅓ cup sugar

Topping:

1 cup Fudge Sauce (page 148)**

½ cup 70% cacao chocolate chips

*Any brownie mix of your choice can be substituted.
**Any commercial hot fudge sauce may be substituted.

Instructions

1. Preheat oven to 350°F. Line 12 muffin/cupcake cups with paper liners. I use Revol crumpled espresso-sized cups for this recipe.

2. Mix all brownie ingredients till well blended.

3. In a separate bowl, mix all cheesecake ingredients till well blended. The cheesecake mixture will be very thick!

4. Pour brownie batter in each cup, filling about halfway full (an ice cream scoop works well for this). Put a dollop of cheesecake filling on top of batter in each brownie cup (I found about 2 teaspoons was the right amount to distribute it evenly between each cup). Top each brownie with about 1 to 2 teaspoons of remaining brownie batter.

5. Bake at 350°F for 20 to 25 minutes, or until cake tester comes out clean. If you are going to bake in the Revol crumpled espresso cups, you will have to bake for 30 to 35 minutes.

6. Microwave the fudge sauce until it's a consistency you can drizzle (about 20 seconds).

7. Drizzle liberally over each cupcake and the messier it looks, the better. Top with chocolate chips.

PRETZEL BROWNIES WITH CARAMEL PEANUT BUTTER SAUCE

A great way to use those leftover pretzels from snacking! Starts with a boxed brownie mix, which is on many pantry shelves.

Serves: 9

Ingredients

1 package (18–19-ounce) brownie mix plus ingredients listed on the package

2–3 cups mini salted pretzels

Caramel Peanut Butter Sauce:

½ cup creamy peanut butter

½ cup heavy cream

¼ cup brown sugar

2 tablespoons light corn syrup

Instructions

1. Preheat oven as per brownie package directions.
2. Spray or grease a 9 x 9-inch baking dish.
3. Prepare brownie mix per package directions, then pour and spread half the batter into the prepared pan.
4. Add a layer of pretzels so almost the entire surface is covered with pretzels.
5. Pour and spread remaining half of the brownie batter over the pretzels, and bake as per package directions.
6. Remove from oven and cool on a rack.
7. Prepare caramel sauce: Mix peanut butter, heavy cream, brown sugar, and corn syrup in a small saucepan.
8. Heat over medium heat until sugar is dissolved and bubbles form around the edge of the sauce.
9. Cut the brownies into squares and serve with warm syrup.

QUICKIE CHOCOLATE–COVERED COOKIE BARS

When the kiddos or grown ups hanker for some candy bars, these are made in a jiffy with what you have on hand and are far cheaper than regular candy bars!

Serves: 4

Ingredients

7–9 whole graham crackers

½ cup caramel sauce

1 cup semi-sweet chocolate chips

2 tablespoons butter

1 tablespoon coarse sea salt

Instructions

1. Line an 8 x 8-inch or 9 x 9-inch pan with aluminum foil.
2. Lay out a layer of graham crackers along the bottom. Fill in spaces with pieces of graham crackers so the bottom is totally covered.
3. Microwave caramel sauce on high for 20 seconds, or until it's a thinner, pourable consistency. Pour over graham crackers, and spread in an even layer.
4. Top with the rest of the graham crackers, repeating as in the first layer, with all the spaces filled.
5. Microwave chocolate chips and butter on high for 1 minute. Remove and stir until very smooth. Spread chocolate over top. Chill.
6. Top with coarse salt and cut into pieces of desired size.

CHOCOLATE-DIPPED ALMOND BISCOTTI

This basic biscotti is easy to make from things you already have! Makes an elegant presentation.

Makes: 9 biscotti

Ingredients

2 eggs

⅔ cup sugar

1 teaspoon salt

2 teaspoons almond extract

1 teaspoon baking powder

1 cup flour

Chocolate Dip:

1¼ cups dark chocolate chips

1 tablespoon shortening

½ cup toasted sliced almonds for coating

Instructions

1. Preheat oven to 370°F. Grease or spray a 9 x 5-inch loaf pan.

2. Beat eggs and sugar well. Add salt, almond extract, and baking powder; beat well. Add the flour and beat until mixed. Pour batter into prepared pan. Bake for 20 to 25 minutes. Remove from oven and cool on rack for about 30 minutes. Remove from pan and slice loaf into 1-inch slices.

3. Heat oven to 400°F.

4. Place biscotti side down on an ungreased baking sheet. Toast about 5 minutes each side. *Watch carefully* as you don't want them to burn. Remove from oven and let cool on the baking sheet overnight to dry.

   NOTE: What I do to speed this process is let the oven cool down slightly and put the sheet with the biscotti back in the oven (the oven is off) and leave them in there until I'm ready to dip them.

5. Prepare chocolate dip by placing chocolate chips and shortening in a microwave-proof bowl. Microwave on high for 1 minute; stir. Microwave for an additional 30 seconds. Stir well until no lumps are in the dip.

6. Line a baking sheet with wax paper.

7. Dip the biscotti halfway down in the chocolate; let excess chocolate drain off. Roll the chocolate portion in the toasted almonds. Place biscotti on prepared baking sheet. Repeat with remaining biscotti.

8. Let chocolate set until firm.

LINDA'S CHOCOLATE PEANUT BUTTER SURPRISE COOKIES

A chocolate cookie with a surprise inside. Reese's lovers, this is your cookie!

Makes: about 2 dozen cookies

Ingredients

Chocolate Cookie:

½ cup butter, softened

½ cup granulated sugar

½ cup packed dark brown sugar

¼ cup creamy peanut butter

1 large egg

1 tablespoon milk

1 teaspoon vanilla extract

1½ cups all-purpose flour

½ cup unsweetened cocoa powder

½ teaspoon baking soda

2 tablespoons granulated sugar

Peanut Butter Center:

¾ cup sifted confectioner's sugar

½ cup creamy peanut butter

Instructions

1. Preheat oven to 350°F.

2. For chocolate cookie: In large mixing bowl, cream together butter, granulated sugar, brown sugar, and creamy peanut butter until combined. Add egg, milk, and vanilla and beat well.

3. Mix together in smaller bowl the flour, cocoa, baking soda, then add to creamed mixture and beat in as much as you can with your mixer. Stir in remaining dry mix with wooden spoon. Form the chocolate dough into a ball about 1¼ inches in diameter. Set aside.

4. For peanut butter center: In medium mixing bowl combine confectioner's sugar and peanut butter until smooth. Shape this mix into ¾-inch balls.

5. On a work surface, slightly flatten chocolate dough ball and put the peanut butter ball in the middle of it. Shape the chocolate dough over the peanut butter filling and completely cover it. Roll into a ball and place on ungreased cookie sheet about 2 inches apart. Lightly flatten cookies with the bottom of a glass dipped in granulated sugar.

6. Bake for 8 minutes until they are set and slightly cracked. Remove from oven and let them stand for a minute or two before removing them to wire racks to cool.

SOPAPILLA CRESCENTS

These delightful cheesecake crescents are made with things you probably have on hand. They're heaven with a cup of good strong coffee!

Serves: 8

Ingredients

6 ounces softened cream cheese (low fat can be subbed)

2 tablespoons sugar

1 tube crescent roll dough

3 tablespoons toasted sliced almonds

2 tablespoons butter, melted

1 tablespoon sugar

¼ teaspoon cinnamon

Instructions

1. Preheat oven to 350°F. Spray or grease the bottom of either an 8 x 8-inch or 9 x 9-inch pan.

2. Beat the softened cream cheese with the sugar until very smooth.

3. Unroll the crescent dough and separate into 8 individual triangles.

4. Divide the cream cheese mixture evenly among the 8 triangles and spread the mixture over the entire triangle. Sprinkle with the toasted almonds reserving about 1 tablespoon for topping. Roll up each triangle the same way you would to make a crescent roll.

5. Place 4 rolls evenly down one side of the pan; place the other 4 rolls evenly down the other side of the pan. (The placement should look like 2 columns of a newspaper.)

6. Mix the 1 tablespoon sugar with the cinnamon. Brush the tops of each crescent roll with the butter. Sprinkle with the cinnamon sugar and remaining toasted almonds.

7. Bake 25 to 30 minutes, or until golden brown, then remove from pan and cool.

8. May be eaten warm or chilled.

LINZER TARTS

This popular Christmas cookie is made from shelf ingredients. Oh so good!

Makes: 6 very large cookies

Ingredients

1 cup very soft unsalted butter*

½ cup sugar

1 large egg

½ teaspoon almond extract

2¼ cups flour

½ cup raspberry preserves

1 cup powdered sugar

*You may substitute regular salted butter in a pinch but do *not* substitute margarine or butter-flavored Crisco.

Instructions

1. Beat butter and sugar until light and fluffy. Add egg and almond extract. Beat well. Add the flour and beat at low speed until a dough forms. Form dough into a ball and place in a plastic bag. Refrigerate for 2 hours.

2. Preheat oven to 375°F.

3. Roll out dough to ⅛-inch thickness. Cut circles with a 3-inch diameter cookie cutter. Cut smaller holes in the center of *half* the cookies with a smaller cookie cutter or even a bottle cap.

4. Place on ungreased cookie sheet and bake for 7 to 10 minutes or until cookies are set and just beginning to get light golden brown around the edges. Cool for 1 minute on the sheet and then remove to a rack to cool completely.

5. When cookies are completely cool, spread about 1 table-spoon of the raspberry preserves on the circles without the additional holes, and spread the jam on the side that was sitting on the cookie sheet because that is completely flat.

6. Top with a cookie with the hole in the center, again placing the side that was on the cookie sheet on the jam, forming a sandwich. Dust with powdered sugar.

BROWN SUGAR SHORTBREAD

Just three ordinary ingredients make this scrumptious shortbread. If you don't have dark brown sugar, use light brown and they'll be just as good.

Makes: 40 cookies

Ingredients

1 cup butter, softened

½ cup dark brown sugar

2¼ cups flour

Instructions

1. Preheat oven to 300°F .

2. Cream butter and sugar in a large bowl. Gradually stir in flour and mix well.

3. Turn dough out onto lightly floured surface and knead until smooth.

4. Place dough on cookie sheet and pat into a rectangle about ⅓-inches thick measuring approximately 8 x 11 inches.

5. Cut into 2-inch by 1-inch pieces. Prick each piece with fork.

6. Bake for about 25 minutes, or until bottoms begin to get lightly brown.

7. Cool on sheet 5 minutes, then remove to rack to cool completely.

CARAMEL GRAHAM CRACKER PARFAIT

So simple yet so good! Serve this one to company, but never let on that it's made from ingredients you probably already have!

Serves: 4

Ingredients

1 box instant butterscotch pudding mix

1¾ cups milk

2 whole graham crackers

½ cup butterscotch morsels

1 teaspoon vegetable shortening (like Crisco—don't use butter or margarine)

2 cups whipped topping

½ cup caramel sauce

Instructions

1. Place pudding mix and milk in a medium bowl and whisk with a wire whisk for 1 minute. Refrigerate until set, about 1 hour.

2. Place graham crackers on a sheet of waxed paper. Melt butterscotch morsels and shortening in a microwave in a microwave-safe bowl for 1 minute on high; stir until no lumps remain. If there are lumps, microwave on high an additional 30 seconds. Pour melted butterscotch over graham crackers, spread to coat evenly. Chill until butterscotch is set.

3. Fold 1 cup of butterscotch pudding into the whipped topping. Break the butterscotch-coated graham crackers into small pieces.

4. In parfait or dessert cups, layer as follows, dividing evenly between 4 dessert cups: plain pudding (about 2 tablespoons), caramel sauce (about 1 tablespoon), graham bits (about 1 tablespoon), whipped topping mixture (about 3 tablespoons).

5. Repeat once more in all dessert cups

6. Decorate top with a dollop of whipped topping and any remaining graham bits.

7. Drizzle remaining caramel sauce over the top.

CHOCOLATE ALMOND CHEESECAKE PARFAIT

This dessert is dedicated to my friend Lillian who loves anything Almond Joy. Nothing exotic here. Made with common ingredients that are in your fridge or pantry.

Serves: 4

Ingredients

1 cup ready-made chocolate sauce or ganache

8 ounces cream cheese, softened

1¼ cups evaporated milk (don't reconstitute)

1 package (4-serving size) coconut cream instant pudding*

1 cup shredded coconut

1 teaspoon coconut extract, or 1 teaspoon vanilla

1 cup whipped topping

¼ cup toasted almonds, sliced

Extra shredded coconut and toasted almonds for garnish

*Vanilla pudding may be substituted if you can't find the coconut variety. The pudding is used dry. *Do not* prepare it as per package directions!

Instructions

1. Place about 2 tablespoons of the chocolate sauce in the bottom of each dessert dish (juice glasses or small wine glasses work well for this dessert).

2. In a large bowl, beat the cream cheese with ¼ cup of the evaporated milk until smooth.

3. Add the pudding, coconut, extract and the remaining evaporated milk. Beat for about 1 minute.

4. Stir in whipped topping and almonds. Spoon into prepared dishes.

5. Chill for about 1 hour.

6. Microwave chocolate sauce or ganache for about 20 seconds or until it's a consistency that will drizzle.

7. Drizzle chocolate sauce over the top of each dessert. Garnish with additional coconut and toasted almonds.

PUMPKIN TURTLE CHEESECAKE PARFAIT

Great dessert for the holidays or any time. It's easy to make and good to have on hand at Thanksgiving for those who don't care for traditional pumpkin pie.

Serves: 4

Ingredients

8 ounces cream cheese, at room temperature

½ cup milk/cream/half-and-half, divided

1 cup pumpkin purée

1 teaspoon pumpkin pie spice

1 package (serves 4) instant vanilla pudding*

8 ounces (1 regular tub) whipped topping

Chopped pecans for garnish

Caramel sauce for drizzle

*The pudding is used dry. *Do not make per package instructions.*

Instructions

1. Beat cream cheese and ¼ cup of the milk/cream in a large bowl until it's smooth and silky.

2. Add the pumpkin, pumpkin pie spice, the remaining milk, and the dry pudding mix. Beat for 1 minute.

3. Fold in whipped topping. Divide evenly into small dessert dishes.

4. Garnish with chopped pecans and drizzle with caramel sauce.

WHITE CHOCOLATE STRAWBERRY CHEESECAKE PARFAIT

Want a quick dessert? Here it is, using ingredients from your freezer and your cupboard shelf. If you don't have cheesecake pudding mix, use vanilla!

Serves: 4

Ingredients

8 ounces cream cheese, softened

1 cup milk

1 package (4 servings size) white chocolate flavored instant pudding

2 cups fresh strawberries, chopped

4 ounces (½ regular-size tub) whipped topping

Instructions

1. Beat cream cheese with an electric mixer in a large bowl.

2. Gradually add milk and beat until mixture is smooth. Add the pudding and beat for 1 minute.

3. Fold in the strawberries and whipped topping.

4. Place in refrigerator and chill for at least 2 hours.

NO-BAKE BLUEBERRY CHEESECAKE

Uses baking staples you have right in the fridge and cupboard.
So creamy, you'll think it's baked!

Serves: 9

Ingredients

½ cup plus 2 tablespoons light cream or half-and-half

⅛ tablespoon unflavored gelatin

2 packages (8-ounce each) cream cheese, softened

¼ cup plus 2 tablespoons confectioner's sugar

½ teaspoon vanilla extract

Crust:

1 cup graham cracker crumbs

5 tablespoons butter, melted

Topping:

1 can (21-ounce) blueberry (or any flavor you like) pie filling

Instructions

1. Mix crust ingredients and press into a 9 x 9-inch pan. Set aside.

2. Place ½ cup of the cream in a microwave safe container. Sprinkle the unflavored gelatin over the cream. Let sit for 5 minutes, then microwave on high for about 30 seconds or until cream is very hot. Stir well to dissolve the gelatin.

3. Place softened cream cheese in a medium bowl and beat with an electric mixer until smooth. Add the confectioner's sugar and vanilla.

   NOTE: I found ¼ cup plus 2 tablespoon of confectioner's sugar was the right amount of sweet for me, but start out at 3 tablespoon or ¼ cup and taste it, adding more If you need it—there are no raw eggs so you won't get sick tasting the filling!

4. Add the cream-gelatin mixture and the remaining 2 tablespoons of cream and beat until light, fluffy, and smooth (the secret to the great texture).

5. Pour filling over the crust and refrigerate until well chilled and set.

6. Spread desired amount of pie filling on top and cut into bars.

CINNAMON BUN ROLLS WITH ORANGE "KIST" ICING

Great for breakfast, dessert, or any time! The hint of orange gives these rolls and icing a very special flavor.

Makes: 12 rolls

Ingredients

Dough:

1 cup lukewarm milk

⅓ cup very soft unsalted butter, cut into pieces

½ cup sugar

2 eggs

1¾ teaspoons salt

2½ teaspoons instant (SAF) yeast or bread machine yeast

4¾ cups all-purpose flour

Filling:

⅓ cup unsalted butter, softened

2 tablespoons cinnamon

1 cup light brown sugar

2 teaspoons orange zest

Icing:

3 ounces cream cheese, softened

¼ cup unsalted butter, softened

1½ cups confectioner's sugar

½ teaspoon orange extract

Instructions

1. Lightly grease a 9 x 13-inch baking pan. Set aside.

2. Combine all dough ingredients in the bowl of a heavy-duty stand mixer. Mix until a soft dough forms. To knead by machine, change mixing paddle to the dough hook and knead for 4 to 7 minutes, or knead by hand 5 to 8 minutes. Dough should be soft but not sticky.*

3. Place about 1 teaspoon of oil in the bottom of a large bowl. Add dough, coat bottom of dough with oil, then turn oil-side up and cover with a greased sheet of plastic wrap.

4. Set in a warm, draft-free place to rise until doubled, about 1½ to 2 hours, depending on conditions. Once risen, punch down dough. Lightly oil your work surface. Turn out dough onto prepared work surface and roll into a rectangle 12 x 16 inches, then spread the butter evenly across the top of the dough.

5. Mix the cinnamon, brown sugar, and orange zest in a small bowl. Sprinkle evenly across buttered surface, then roll up tightly starting from narrow end. Seal seam. Cut into 12 slices, 1-inch thick. Place in prepared baking pan 3 slices across short end, 4 slices down long end.

6. Cover with greased plastic wrap and set in a warm, draft-free place to rise until doubled in size, about 45 to 60 minutes.

7. Preheat oven to 375°F. Bake for 20 to 25 minutes, or until rolls are golden brown on the top.

8. While rolls are baking, prepare icing by placing cream cheese and butter in a medium bowl. Beat the butter and cream cheese well, then add the confectioner's sugar, ½ cup at a time, beating until smooth. Add the orange extract and beat until well blended.

9. Ice rolls while still very warm. Serve warm or cooled.

* To make dough in a bread machine, add dough ingredients per bread maker's instructions. Run on DOUGH cycle and let rise in the machine.

RASPBERRY BUTTER CRUMB CAKE

A made-from-scratch cake from basic on-hand ingredients that's easier to make than a box mix. You can't beat that!

Serves: 9

Ingredients

Crumbs:

4 tablespoons unsalted butter

¼ cup packed brown sugar

½ cup sugar

¼ teaspoon salt

1 teaspoon cinnamon

1 cup plus 2 tablespoons flour

Cake:

1 cup flour

½ cup sugar

1¾ teaspoons baking powder

1 teaspoon salt

½ cup milk

6 tablespoons unsalted butter, melted

1 egg

½ cup raspberry jam (or flavor of your choice)

Instructions

1. Preheat oven to 400°F. Grease a 9-inch pan (square or round).

2. For crumbs: Melt the butter in either a microwave-safe dish or in a small saucepan; remove from heat, if cooking on a stovetop.

3. Stir in the sugars, salt, and cinnamon; combine well. Add the flour and stir to combine well. It's best to work this with your fingers after the flour is stirred in, as the crumbs seem to form better. Set aside.

4. For cake: In a large bowl, combine the flour, sugar, baking powder and salt. Stir well.

5. In a smaller bowl, whisk together the milk, melted butter and the egg.

6. Stir the milk mixture into the flour mixture until just combined. Don't overmix! Pour into prepared pan. Drop teaspoonfuls of raspberry jam randomly over the top of the batter. Swirl gently with a spoon to create a slight marbling effect. Don't fully combine the jam and the batter.

7. Top with crumbs. Bake at 400°F for 25 minutes or until toothpick inserted in center (of cake batter) comes out clean.

8. Cool completely on rack. Dust with confectioner's sugar, if desired.

ABSOLUTELY ALMOND POUND CAKE

The almond pastry filling in this probably isn't an item you have on the shelf, but it's worth picking some up on your next grocery visit because it lasts forever. Pastry filling comes in a can and it's <u>not</u> the same thing as almond paste or marzipan so be careful when selecting.

Makes: 1 cake

Ingredients

2¼ cups flour

½ teaspoon salt

2 teaspoons baking powder

1 cup butter, softened

1 cup sugar

3 eggs

1 can almond pastry filling (such as Solo)

¼ cup milk

Glaze:

1 cup confectioner's sugar

¼ teaspoon almond extract

2 tablespoons light cream or half-and-half

Instructions

1. Preheat oven to 350°F. Grease or spray a Bundt or tube pan. Mix flour, salt, and baking powder in a medium bowl.

2. Cream butter and sugar until light and fluffy. Add eggs, one at a time, beating well after each addition. Add almond pastry filling; beat well.

3. Add flour mixture and milk to wet ingredients, alternating and ending with the flour. Scrape down sides and blend well.

4. Place batter in prepared pan, spreading evenly. Bake for 50 to 55 minutes or until cake tester inserted in center comes out clean.

5. Remove from oven and cool in pan for 10 minutes. Invert on a rack to cool completely.

6. Prepare glaze by mixing confectioner's sugar and almond extract. Add cream, 1 tablespoon at a time until consistency of a thick but pourable glaze. Drizzle completely cooled cake with glaze. Let glaze set (maybe 15 or so minutes) before slicing.

PEACH CRISP (AKA "THE PEACH THING")

Truly a cupboard-item dessert. Frozen, fresh, or canned peaches can be used.

Serves: 4

Ingredients

10 ounce frozen peaches (no sugar added), defrosted

¼ cup sugar

¼ teaspoon cinnamon or allspice

4 tablespoons flour, divided

1 cup quick oats

2 tablespoons cold butter

2 tablespoons sugar

2 tablespoons brown sugar

Instructions

1. Preheat oven to 350°F. Spray 4 individual casserole dishes (ramekins) with nonstick spray (you can use a 1-quart casserole dish as well).

2. Mix peaches with sugar, cinnamon, and 1 tablespoon flour. Set aside.

3. In a separate bowl, combine oats, butter, sugar, and 3 tablespoons flour, cutting in butter until it's the size of small peas.

4. Place peaches in prepared pans. Top with oatmeal crumbs and sprinkle with the brown sugar.

5. Bake for 30 to 40 minutes, or until fruit juice begins bubbling from the sides of the casserole and the crumbs are lightly browned.

NOTE: You can substitute whole-wheat flour for the white in this for extra nutrition and fiber.

APPLE FLAUTAS

Got tortillas and a can of pie filling? Then you've got this spectacular dessert covered!

Serves: 6

Ingredients

6 tablespoons butter

6 small (6-inch) flour tortillas

¼ cup plus 2 tablespoons cinnamon sugar (3 parts sugar to 1 part ground cinnamon)

2 cups apple pie filling (1 large can)

¼ cup caramel sauce or dulce de leche

Powdered sugar (optional)

Instructions

1. Preheat oven to 350°F.

2. Melt 4 tablespoons of butter in a 10-inch skillet. Dip one side of a tortilla in the melted butter and place buttered side up on a baking sheet.

3. Sprinkle buttered side with cinnamon sugar, turn, and brush other side of tortilla with butter, then sprinkle with cinnamon sugar. Repeat with all tortillas.

4. Place tortillas in preheated oven for about 5 minutes, or until they are pliable enough to roll.

5. Roll tortillas into a loose roll and place seam-side down on baking sheet.

6. Return to oven and bake for 10 to 15 minutes, or until tortillas are crispy and begin to brown. Remove from oven; place on serving platter and set aside.

7. Melt 2 tablespoons of butter in a 10-inch skillet over medium heat. When butter begins to brown, add pie filling and 2 tablespoons cinnamon sugar. Stir until sugar is dissolved and mixture begins to boil.

8. Spoon hot apple mixture on top of rolled tortillas. Drizzle with caramel sauce. May be dusted with powdered sugar if desired. Serve immediately.

APPLE PIE COOKIES

Now here's something you can make from scraps of pastry and left-over pie filling! They are a bit fussy, but make a lovely presentation when served with coffee or tea.

Makes 1 giant 10-inch cookie or about 6 smaller cookies
(with odd-shaped extras)

Ingredients

2 ready-made refrigerated piecrusts

1 can (21-ounce) apple pie filling

1 egg

1 tablespoon water

¼ cup sugar

½ teaspoon cinnamon

Flour, for dusting

½ cup caramel sauce

Instructions

1. Preheat oven to 350°F. Line a large baking sheet with parchment paper or use a non-stick sheet. (Parchment is highly recommended.)

2. Bring crusts to room temperature as per package instructions.

3. Chop the apple pie filling so the apples are in small chunks. You don't want the big slices. I used my food processor for this task.

4. Beat the egg with the water in a small bowl. Mix the sugar and cinnamon in another bowl.

5. Dust your work surface with a little bit of flour. Carefully unroll one of the piecrusts and place on the lightly floured surface. Using a rolling pin, roll the dough very gently until it's just slightly thinner. Spread the caramel sauce over the entire crust. Spread the processed pie filling on top of the caramel sauce.

6. Carefully roll out the second crust and place that on a lightly floured surface. Roll the same way as the first crust, just slightly thinner.

7. Using a pastry wheel or pizza cutter, cut this crust into (approximately) ½-inch strips. This is for the lattice top. Form lattice over the top of the filled crust.

8. Using a round cookie cutter that's about 2 to 3 inches in diameter, cut individual "cookies" and, using a spatula to lift them, place on prepared baking sheet. There will be "bitsies" left over. Bake them up too . . . not as pretty but just as good. You can eliminate the cookie cutting step and just make a giant cookie. That way you don't get the odd "bitsies."

9. Brush the tops of each cookie with the egg wash. Sprinkle each cookie with the cinnamon sugar and bake for 25 to 30 minutes or until lattice tops are golden brown. Cool slightly and remove to a rack or plate to cool further. These may be eaten warm.

FRIED JAM PIES

Have any variety jam in the fridge? Have pastry scraps in the fridge or freezer? You have what it takes to make these!

Makes: 8 mini pies per 1 ready-made piecrust

Ingredients

1–2 refrigerated ready-made piecrusts, or piecrust scraps

Oil for frying

½ cup (approximate) any flavor jam or preserves

Confectioner's sugar

Instructions

1. Unroll refrigerated piecrusts. If using scraps, roll out to about 1/8-inch thickness.

2. Use a 3-inch diameter round cookie cutter (or glass or jar lid of same size) to cut circles of crust. Gather scraps, roll out again, repeat the cutting.

3. Heat about ½ inch of oil in a heavy skillet to 350°F. Oil will shimmer when it gets to the right frying temperature.

4. Place about 1 teaspoon of jam in the center of each circle. Wet finger with water and dampen the outside rim of each circle. Fold crust over, making a half-moon shape. Seal edges with a fork.

5. Place pies in hot oil (don't overcrowd them in pan—fry in batches if necessary). Fry each side about 1 minute, or until golden brown.

6. Remove from pan and drain on a plate lined with paper towels. Cool completely. Dust with powdered sugar and serve.

CLASSIC PUMPKIN PIE

A timeless classic. Who doesn't have all it takes to make one of these around the holidays? Stock up on canned pumpkin when it's on sale, then you can make it year round.

Makes: 1 pie

Ingredients

2 eggs

1¾ cups pumpkin purée

¾ cup sugar

1 teaspoon cinnamon

½ teaspoon ground ginger

¼ teaspoon ground cloves

1 (12-ounce) can evaporated milk

1 unbaked 9-inch pie shell

Instructions

1. Preheat oven to 425°F.

2. In a large bowl, beat eggs. Add pumpkin, sugar, and spices; beat well. Gradually stir in evaporated milk.

3. Place pie shell on baking sheet, place in oven, then pour filling into the pie shell.

4. Bake for 15 minutes, then reduce temperature to 350°F and bake for an additional 40 to 50 minutes, or until knife inserted near center comes out clean.

5. Cool completely on rack. Chill if desired.

LEMON SQUARES

If you juice and zest lemons and place each in the freezer, you'll have what it takes to make these popular dessert bars.

Makes: 24 large squares

Ingredients

Crust:

2 cups flour

½ cup confectioner's sugar

Pinch salt

1 cup butter

Filling:

4 eggs

½ cup lemon juice

¼ cup flour

1½ cups sugar

Zest of 1 lemon

Instructions

1. Mix the flour, confectioner's sugar, and salt in a mixing bowl. Cut in butter.

2. Lightly spray a 9 x 13-inch baking pan. Add crust mixture and spread evenly over pan, pressing down firmly.

3. Bake in preheated 350°F oven 15 to 20 minutes or until edges are light golden brown.

4. While crust is baking, make filling. Beat eggs until thick and foamy. Add remaining filling ingredients and beat well. Pour filling over hot crust.

5. Return to oven and bake for 20 minutes or until filling is set.

6. Cool completely. Cut into squares with wet knife to prevent tearing. Dust with powdered sugar before serving.

ORANGE CREAMSICLES

You might have to buy some Greek yogurt for this one, but Greek yogurt is always good to have on hand because it's a good substitute for a few common ingredients.

Makes: 10 pops (approximately)

Ingredients

1½ cups Greek yogurt

¼ cup sugar

½ cup cream

¼ cup milk

¼ teaspoon vanilla

1 package (12 fluid ounces) orange juice concentrate, thawed

Instructions

1. Process all ingredients, except for orange juice concentrate, in a blender.

2. Spoon about 1 to 2 tablespoons (depending on the size of your popsicle molds) of orange juice concentrate in each mold.

3. Top this with about 2 to 3 tablespoons of the yogurt mixture (again it depends on the size of your mold).

4. Repeat until molds are filled, leaving a bit of space at the top to allow for expansion during freezing (maybe ¹⁄₁₆ to ⅛ of an inch).

5. Cover mold, add sticks, and freeze for at least 6 hours or overnight.

SPIKED BLACKBERRY ICE CREAM

An adults-only ice cream! Adding a bit of alcohol stops it from freezing hard as a rock. Leave out the booze for the kiddos and teetotalers. It's a great ice cream either way.

Serves: 4

Ingredients

2 cups fresh or frozen (defrosted) blackberries

¼ cup sugar

¼ cup liquor of your choice (I use brandy)

Custard:

4 egg yolks

3 cups heavy cream

1 cup light cream

¾ cup sugar

Instructions

1. Place berries in a medium bowl. Add the sugar and liquor. Using a muddler or a potato masher, mash berries. Cover and refrigerate for later use—ice cream relies on a cooked custard that also must be chilled, so I always do the berries and custard at least a day before I make the actual ice cream.

2. In a small bowl, beat egg yolks. Heat the creams and sugar over medium heat in a 3-quart saucepan, stirring constantly.

3. When custard is hot (do not boil!), take about 1 cup of the cream mixture and whisk it into the egg yolks (tempering), then add back to the cream mixture, whisking the tempered yolks into the cream mixture to incorporate.

4. Stir the mixture constantly until it reaches 160°F, or until mixture coats the back of a spoon—this should take about 5 minutes—again, do *not* let the mixture boil.

5. Remove from heat and cool to room temperature. I stir to prevent a skin from forming; you could also just remove the skin and discard it once the mixture is cooled.

6. When custard is room temp, transfer into a covered container and refrigerate until completely chilled.

7. To make ice cream: Stir the entire contents of the fruit bowl into the chilled custard.

8. Follow directions for your ice cream maker. I use a model with a compressor and it takes about 30 minutes to form soft-serve ice cream. At that point, I transfer to another container to hard freeze, but it can be served soft if you prefer.

P.S. DON'T FORGET THE DRINKS!

JAZZBERRY SMOOTHIE

If you have frozen berries in the freezer and Greek yogurt in the fridge, this is your smoothie! Use any combination of berries. Simply delish!

Serves: 2 (8-ounce) servings

Ingredients

1 cup frozen raspberries

1 cup plain Greek yogurt

2 tablespoons sugar or honey

¾ cup milk

Instructions

1. Place contents in a blender or a deep container, if you are using a stick blender.

2. Process until smooth. Serve immediately.

   Note: For a real taste sensation—this is what can really make it "jazzy"—chop a leaf or two of peppermint in with the fruit. Very nice and cooling.

BLUEBERRY CREME SMOOTHIE

Delicious and rich! Another reason to have Greek yogurt in your fridge!

Serves: 2

Ingredients

1 cup Greek yogurt

½ cup milk

1 cup frozen or fresh blueberries

1 teaspoon flaxseed oil (optional)

¼ cup sugar, honey, agave, stevia, etc. (optional)

Instructions

1. Place contents in a blender or a deep container, if you are using a stick blender.

2. Process until smooth. Serve immediately.

   Note: This does taste nice with a bit of mint. I only used it as a garnish but what I licked off the leaves (yes, I am a slob) tasted great!

DULCE DE LECHE SMOOTHIE

Have dulce de leche on hand? Make this delicious and different smoothie.

Serves: 2

Ingredients

1 cup low-fat yogurt, plain or vanilla

2 tablespoons dulce de leche

1½ cups milk (any variety will do, I use whole)

Instructions

1. Combine all ingredients in a very deep cup. I use the plastic cup that comes with my immersion blender.

2. Process with immersion blender until dulce de leche is combined well, about 1 minute.

3. Pour into glasses and serve immediately.

BANANA COCONUT SMOOTHIE

Whip this one up nice and easy. It's a different way to use your flavored coffee creamers. Any flavor may be substituted for the coconut.

Serves: 1

Ingredients

½ cup milk

¼ cup half-and-half

2 tablespoons Carnation Coconut Crème coffee creamer

1½ whole bananas, sliced or ½ cup partially frozen mashed

1 tablespoon toasted coconut for topping

Instructions

1. Put all ingredients except the toasted coconut in an immersion (stick) blender bowl—the one that comes with it, or a deep narrow container.

2. Process with immersion blender on high for 1 minute.

3. Pour into serving glass and top with toasted coconut.

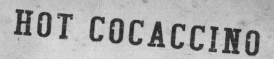

HOT COCACCINO

Be your own barista with ingredients you have on the shelf and in the fridge!

Serves: 2

Ingredients

2 packages hot cocoa mix (like Swiss Miss)

1 cup milk

½ cup half-and-half or light cream

1 teaspoon instant coffee or instant espresso

½ cup mini marshmallows

¼ cup chocolate syrup (I use U-Bet)

Whipped topping or whipped cream for garnish

Sprinkles or sifted cocoa for garnish

Instructions

1. Heat milk and half-and-half in medium saucepan until very hot; remove from heat.

2. Add hot cocoa mix and instant coffee. Stir well and pour into mugs or cups.

3. Top with mini marshmallows, then drizzle chocolate syrup over marshmallows. Top with whipped topping and sprinkles or cocoa powder.

INDEX

A

Absolutely Almond Pound Cake, 176–177

Acorn Squash Cups, 88–89

Aloha Pineapple Chicken, 40–41

Amish White Bread, 123

appetizers. *See* snacks and starters

apples

Apple Butter BBQ Ribs, 58–59

Apple Flautas, 180–181

Apple Pie Cookies, 182–183

Apricot Chicken, 42–43

Asiago Spinach Dip, Hot, 12–13

Asian Spinach, 95

B

bacon

Bacon Bombs, 4–5

Bacon Cheeseburger Meatloaf, 24–25

Bacon Cheese Pull-Aparts, 120–121

Classic Cheddar Bacon Macaroni & Cheese, 72–73

Baked Golden Ranch Pork Chops, 60–61

bananas

Banana Coconut Smoothie, 202

Chocolate Chip Banana Bread, 136–137

BBQ Ribs, Apple Butter, 58–59

beef, ground

Bacon Cheeseburger Meatloaf, 24–25

Deluxe Skillet Taco Pie, 28–29

Meatball Subs, 32–33

One-Skillet Salisbury Steak with Butter Merlot Sauce, 34–35

Skillet Beef Pasta Caprese with Fire-Roasted Tomatoes, 38–39

Taco Cups, 20–21

Takeout Beef Fried Rice, 30–31

beef roast, Classic Pot Roast, 28–29

beef sirloin, Rustic Beef Pot Pie, 36–37

Beer Batter Onion Rings, 90–91

bell peppers

Corn Relish, 102

Quinoa-Stuffed Peppers, 82–83

Shrimp Newburg, 77

berries

Blueberry Creme Smoothie, 198–199

Jazzberry Smoothie, 196–197

No-Bake Blueberry Cheesecake, 170–171

Raspberry Butter Crumb Cake, 174–175

Spiked Blackberry Ice Cream, 192–193

Strawberry Spice Muffins, 140–141

Sylvia's Cranberry Orange Bread, 134–135

White Chocolate Strawberry Cheesecake Parfait, 168–169

beverages, Hot Cocaccino, 203

Biscuits & Sausage Gravy Pot Pie, 62–63

Blueberry Cheesecake, No-Bake, 170–171

Blueberry Creme Smoothie, 198–199

Bourbon-Glazed Pork Chops, 64–65

bread

Amish White Bread, 123

Bacon Cheese Pull-Aparts, 120–121

Cheesy Onion Monkey Bread, 122

Chocolate Chip Banana Bread, 136–137

Easy Hawaiian Rolls, 126–127

Easy Irish Soda Bread, 124–125

bread (*continued*)

    Honey Wheat Bread, 128–129

    Lemon-Lime Soda Biscuits, 130–131

    Poblano & Cheese Cornbread, 132–133

    Sylvia's Cranberry Orange Bread, 134–135

broccoli

    Cheesy Broccoli Rice Casserole, 96–97

    Cream of Broccoli Cheddar Soup, 100–101

Brown Sugar Shortbread, 161

Brussels Sprouts, Roasted Maple, 112–113

C

cake

    Absolutely Almond Pound Cake, 176–177

    Raspberry Butter Crumb Cake, 174–175

    . *See also* cheesecake

Caramel Graham Cracker Parfait, 6, 162–163

Carrot & Raisin Salad, 94

casseroles

    Cheesy Broccoli Rice Casserole, 96–97

    Chicken Cordon Bleu Casserole, 46–47

cheese

    Bacon Cheeseburger Meatloaf, 24–25

    Bacon Cheese Pull-Aparts, 120–121

    Cajun Smoked Sausage Alfredo, 66–67

    Cheesy Broccoli Rice Casserole, 96–97

    Cheesy Onion Monkey Bread, 122

    Cheesy Pretzel Bites, 6–7

    Chicken Cordon Bleu Casserole, 46–47

    Chicken Crescent Bake, 48–49

    Classic Cheddar Bacon Macaroni & Cheese, 72–73

    Clean-the-Fridge Quiche, 85

    Cream of Broccoli Cheddar Soup, 100–101

    Deluxe Skillet Taco Pie, 28–29

    Egg Baskets, 78–79

    Fake Lasagna, 68–69

    Garlic Asiago Fingerling Potatoes, 106–107

    Hot Asiago Spinach Dip, 12–13

    Italian Herb Chicken with Roasted Vegetables, 50–51

    Linguine with Toasted Pecan Arugula Pesto, 80–81

    Meatball Subs, 32–33

    Parmesan Garlic Snack Mix, 14–15

    Pasta and Green Bean Salad with Lemon Tarragon Dressing, 110–111

    Pasta with Mushrooms & Basil, 84

    Pepperjack Chicken, 54–55

    Pepperoni Pizza Pull-Apart, 18

    Poblano & Cheese Cornbread, 132–133

    Quinoa-Stuffed Peppers, 82–83

    Ricotta Lemon Poppy Muffins, 142–143

    Scalloped Potatoes Gratin, 116–117

    Skillet Beef Pasta Caprese with Fire-Roasted Tomatoes, 38–39

    Taco Cups, 20–21

    . *See also* cream cheese

cheesecake

    Chocolate Almond Cheesecake Parfait, 164–165

    Death by Chocolate Cheesecake Brownie Cups, 149

    No-Bake Blueberry Cheesecake, 170–171

    Pumpkin Turtle Cheesecake Parfait, 166–167

    White Chocolate Strawberry Cheesecake Parfait, 168–169

chicken

    Aloha Pineapple Chicken, 40–41

    Apricot Chicken, 42–43

    Asian Chicken Thighs, 44–45

    Chicken Cordon Bleu Casserole, 46–47

    Chicken Crescent Bake, 48–49

    Italian Herb Chicken with Roasted Vegetables, 50–51

One-Pan Chicken & Orzo Skillet Dinner, 52–53

Pepperjack Chicken, 54–55

Spicy Oven-Fried Chicken, 56–57

chocolate

Chocolate Almond Cheesecake Parfait, 164–165

Chocolate Chip Banana Bread, 136–137

Chocolate Chip Muffins, 138–139

Chocolate-Dipped Almond Biscotti, 154–155

Chocolate Peanut Butter Cookie Dough Bites, 146–147

Death by Chocolate Cheesecake Brownie Cups, 149

Fudge Sauce, 148, 149

Hot Cocaccino, 203

Linda's Chocolate Peanut Butter Surprise Cookies, 156

Pretzel Brownies with Caramel Peanut Butter Sauce, 150–151

Quickie Chocolate-Covered Cookie Bars, 152–153

White Chocolate Strawberry Cheesecake Parfait, 168–169

Chocolate Almond Cheesecake Parfait, 164–165

Cinnamon Bun Rolls with Orange "Kist" Icing, 172–173

Clean-the-Fridge Quiche, 85

Coconut Shrimp, 8–9

Coleslaw, Kicked-up, 109

Comeback Sauce, 92

Cookie Bars, Quickie Chocolate-Covered, 152–153

cookies

Apple Pie, 182–183

Linda's Chocolate Peanut Butter Surprise, 156

Corn Dogs, State Fair, 19

Corn Relish, 102

Cranberry Orange Bread, Sylvia's, 134–135

cream cheese

Bacon Bombs, 4–5

Chicken Crescent Bake, 48–49

Chocolate Almond Cheesecake Parfait, 164–165

Cinnamon Bun Rolls with Orange "Kist" Icing, 172–173

Death by Chocolate Cheesecake Brownie Cups, 149

Fake Lasagna, 68–69

Hot Asiago Spinach Dip, 12–13

No-Bake Blueberry Cheesecake, 170–171

Pumpkin Turtle Cheesecake Parfait, 166–167

Sopapilla Crescents, 157

White Chocolate Strawberry Cheesecake Parfait, 168–169

Cream of Broccoli Cheddar Soup, 100–101

Creole Seasoning Blend, 93

Cucumber Dill Salad, 103

custard, 192

D

Death by Chocolate Cheesecake Brownie Cups, 149

desserts

Absolutely Almond Pound Cake, 176–177

Apple Flautas, 180–181

Apple Pie Cookies, 182–183

Brown Sugar Shortbread, 160–161

Caramel Graham Cracker Parfait, 162–163

Chocolate Almond Cheesecake Parfait, 164–165

Chocolate-Dipped Almond Biscotti, 154–155

Chocolate Peanut Butter Cookie Dough Bites, 146–147

desserts (*continued*)

Cinnamon Bun Rolls with Orange "Kist" Icing, 172–173

Classic Pumpkin Pie, 186–187

Death by Chocolate Cheesecake Brownie Cups, 149

Fried Jam Pies, 184–185

Fudge Sauce, 148, 149

Lemon Square, 188–189

Linda's Chocolate Peanut Butter Surprise Cookies, 156

Linzer Tarts, 158–159

No-Bake Blueberry Cheesecake, 170–171

Orange Creamsicles, 190–191

Peach Crisp (AKA "The Peach Thing"), 178–179

Pretzel Brownies with Caramel Peanut Butter Sauce, 150–151

Pumpkin Turtle Cheesecake Parfait, 166–167

Quickie Chocolate-Covered Cookie Bars, 152–153

Raspberry Butter Crumb Cake, 174–175

Sopapilla Crescents, 157

Spiked Blackberry Ice Cream, 192–193

White Chocolate Strawberry Cheesecake Parfait, 168–169

dressings. *See* sauces and dressings

Dulce de Leche Smoothie, 200–201

E

Egg Baskets, 78–79

F

Fake Lasagna, 68–69

Fiesta Rice with House Special Dressing, 104–105

Fried Jam Pies, 184–185

Fudge Sauce, 148, 149

G

Garlic Asiago Fingerling Potatoes, 106–107

Garlic Lime Wings, 10–11

German Potato Salad, 108

ground pork, Pot Stickers, 16–17

H

Hawaiian Rolls, Easy, 126–127

Honey Wheat Bread, 128–129

Hot Cocaccino, 203

I

Ice Cream, Spiked Blackberry, 192–193

Irish Soda Bread, Easy, 124–125

Italian Herb Chicken with Roasted Vegetables, 50–51

J

Jazzberry Smoothie, 196–197

L

Lasagna, Fake, 68–69

Lemon-Lime Soda Biscuits, 130–131

Lemon Square, 188–189

Linda's Chocolate Peanut Butter Surprise Cookies, 156

Linguine with Toasted Pecan Arugula Pesto, 80–81

Linzer Tarts, 158–159

M

Macaroni & Cheese, Classic Cheddar Bacon, 72–73

Macaroni Salad, Classic, 98–99

main dishes

Aloha Pineapple Chicken, 40–41

Apple Butter BBQ Ribs, 58–59

Apricot Chicken, 42–43

Asian Chicken Thighs, 44–45

Bacon Cheeseburger Meatloaf, 24–25

Baked Golden Ranch Pork Chops, 60–61

Biscuits & Sausage Gravy Pot Pie, 62–63

Bourbon-Glazed Pork Chops, 64–65

Cajun Smoked Sausage Alfredo, 66–67

Chicken Cordon Bleu Casserole, 46–47

Chicken Crescent Bake, 48–49

Classic Cheddar Bacon Macaroni & Cheese,
    72–73

Classic Pot Roast, 26–27

Clean-the-Fridge Quiche, 85

Deluxe Skillet Taco Pie, 28–29

Egg Baskets, 78–79

Fake Lasagna, 68–69

Italian Herb Chicken with Roasted Vegeta-
    bles, 50–51

Linguine with Toasted Pecan Arugula Pesto,
    80–81

Meatball Subs, 32–33

One-Pan Chicken & Orzo Skillet Dinner,
    52–53

One-Skillet Salisbury Steak with Butter Merlot
    Sauce, 34–35

Pasta with Mushrooms & Basil, 84

Pepperjack Chicken, 54–55

Pineapple Cilantro Shrimp, 74–75

Pork Chops with Lemon Thyme Cream Sauce,
    70–71

Quinoa-Stuffed Peppers, 82–83

Rustic Beef Pot Pie, 36–37

Shrimp Newburg, 76–77

Skillet Beef Pasta Caprese with Fire-Roasted
    Tomatoes, 38–39

Spicy Oven-Fried Chicken, 56–57

Takeout Beef Fried Rice, 30–31

Meatball Subs, 32–33

merlot sauce, 34

muffins
    Chocolate Chip Muffins, 138–139
    Ricotta Lemon Poppy Muffins, 142–143
    Strawberry Spice Muffins, 140–141

O

One-Pan Chicken & Orzo Skillet Dinner, 52–53

Onion Monkey Bread, Cheesy, 122

Onion Rings, Beer Batter, 90–91

Orange Creamsicles, 190–191

P

pantry items, 10–11

parfaits
    Caramel Graham Cracker Parfait, 162–163
    Chocolate Almond Cheesecake Parfait,
        164–165
    Pumpkin Turtle Cheesecake Parfait, 166–167
    White Chocolate Strawberry Cheesecake Par-
        fait, 168–169

Parmesan Garlic Snack Mix, 14–15

pasta
    Cajun Smoked Sausage Alfredo, 66–67
    Fake Lasagna, 68–69
    Linguine with Toasted Pecan Arugula Pesto,
        80–81
    Pasta and Green Bean Salad with Lemon Tar-
        ragon Dressing, 110–111
    Pasta with Mushrooms & Basil, 84
    Skillet Beef Pasta Caprese with Fire-Roasted
        Tomatoes, 38–39

Peach Crisp (AKA "The Peach Thing"), 178–179

Pepperjack Chicken, 54–55

Pepperoni Pizza Pull-Apart, 18

pesto, 81

Poblano & Cheese Cornbread, 132–133
pork chops
    Baked Golden Ranch Pork Chops, 60–61
    Bourbon-Glazed Pork Chops, 64–65
    Pork Chops with Lemon Thyme Cream Sauce,
        70–71
potatoes
    Garlic Asiago Fingerling Potatoes, 106–107
    German Potato Salad, 108
    Scalloped Potatoes Gratin, 116–117
pot pies
    Biscuits & Sausage Gravy Pot Pie, 62–63
    Rustic Beef Pot Pie, 36–37
Pot Roast, Classic, 26–27
Pot Stickers, 16–17
pretzels
    Cheesy Pretzel Bites, 6–7
    Pretzel Brownies with Caramel Peanut Butter
        Sauce, 150–151
Pumpkin Pie, Classic, 186–187
Pumpkin Turtle Cheesecake Parfait, 166–167

Q

Quiche, Clean-the-Fridge, 85
Quinoa-Stuffed Peppers, 82–83

R

Raspberry Butter Crumb Cake, 174–175
Ricotta Lemon Poppy Muffins, 142–143
Roasted Maple Brussels Sprouts, 112–113
Rustic Beef Pot Pie, 36–37

S

salad
    Carrot & Raisin Salad, 94
    Classic Macaroni Salad, 98–99
    Cucumber Dill Salad, 103

Fiesta Rice with House Special Dressing,
    104–105
    German Potato Salad, 108
Salisbury Steak with Butter Merlot Sauce,
    One-Skillet, 34–35
sauces and dressings
    Aloha Pineapple Sauce, 41
    Apple Butter BBQ sauce, 58
    Comeback Sauce, 92
    Egg Basket cheese sauce, 78
    Fudge Sauce, 148, 149
    House Special dressing, 105
    Lemon Tarragon dressing, 111
    Lemon Thyme Cream sauce, 70
    Merlot sauce, 34
    Peanut Butter Caramel sauce, 150
    Toasted Pecan Arugula Pesto, 81
    Wing sauce, 10
Scalloped Potatoes Gratin, 116–117
seasonings
    Creole Seasoning Blend, 93
    Spicy Oven-Fried Chicken seasoning mix, 57
shrimp
    Coconut Shrimp, 8–9
    Pineapple Cilantro Shrimp, 74–75
    Shrimp Newburg, 76–77
Skillet Beef Pasta Caprese with Fire-Roasted
    Tomatoes, 38–39
smoothies
    Banana Coconut Smoothie, 202
    Blueberry Creme Smoothie, 198–199
    Dulce de Leche Smoothie, 200–201
    Jazzberry Smoothie, 196–197
snacks and starters
    Bacon Bombs, 4–5
    Cheesy Pretzel Bites, 6–7
    Coconut Shrimp, 8–9

Garlic Lime Wings, 10–11
Hot Asiago Spinach Dip, 12–13
Parmesan Garlic Snack Mix, 14–15
Pepperoni Pizza Pull-Apart, 18
Pot Stickers, 16–17
State Fair Corn Dogs, 19
Taco Cups, 20–21
Sopapilla Crescents, 157
soups and sides
Acorn Squash Cups, 88–89
Asian Spinach, 95
Beer Batter Onion Rings, 90–91
Carrot & Raisin Salad, 94
Cheesy Broccoli Rice Casserole, 96–97
Classic Macaroni Salad, 98–99
Comeback Sauce, 92
Corn Relish, 102
Cream of Broccoli Cheddar Soup, 100–101
Creole Seasoning Blend, 93
Cucumber Dill Salad, 103
Fiesta Rice with House Special Dressing, 104–105
Garlic Asiago Fingerling Potatoes, 106–107
German Potato Salad, 108
Kicked-up Coleslaw, 109

Pasta and Green Bean Salad with Lemon Tarragon Dressing, 110–111
Roasted Maple Brussels Sprouts, 112–113
Scalloped Potatoes Gratin, 116–117
Toasted Israeli Couscous with Mushrooms, 114 115
Spicy Oven-Fried Chicken, 56–57
Spiked Blackberry Ice Cream, 192–193
spinach
Asian Spinach, 95
Hot Asiago Spinach Dip, 12–13
Squash, Acorn Cups, 88–89
Strawberry Spice Muffins, 140–141
Sylvia's Cranberry Orange Bread, 134–135

T
Taco Cups, 20–21
Taco Pie, Deluxe Skillet, 28–29
Takeout Beef Fried Rice, 30–31
Toasted Israeli Couscous with Mushrooms, 114–115

W
White Chocolate Strawberry Cheesecake Parfait, 168–169
wing sauce, 10